BOLIVIA

Robert Pateman & Marcus Cramer

MARSHALL CAVENDISH BENCHMARK

NEW YORK

PICTURE CREDITS
Cover photo: © David Mercado / CORBIS
AFP: 5, 47, 48, 53, 92 • alt.TYPE / Reuters: 32, 33, 54, 88 • Bernard Sonneville: 18, 57, 95, 96, 120 • Bjorn Klingwall: 10, 22, 68, 70 • Camera Press: 20, 34 • David Simson: 77 • Douglas Donne Bryant: 4, 19, 23, 113 • Eye Ubiquitous / Bennett Dean: 50, 51 • Eye Ubiquitous / Hutchison: 94 • HBL Network Photo Agency: 36, 66, 104, 117 • Hulton Deutsch: 24, 82 • Hutchison Library: 14, 21, 58, 83, 129 • Hutchison Library / Eric Lawrie: 115 • Hutchison Library / Mary Jelliffe: 1, 16 • ImageHub: 6, 44 • John Maier: 78, 102, 110, 111 • Liba Taylor: 73, 74 • Life File Photos Ltd: 38, 72, 90 • Lonely Planet Images: 28, 39, 56 • Marka / Fausto Giaccone: 118 • Masterfile / Albert Normandin: 80 • Minden Pictures / Pete Oxford: 46 • National Geographic: 45, 112 • Peter McFarren: 3, 26, 40, 43, 59, 60, 64, 65, 67, 69, 76, 79, 84, 100, 107, 109, 114, 125 • Photobank / Photolibrary: 11, 12, 116, 122, 127 • Richard I'Anson: 7, 15, 30, 42, 87, 93 • Robert Pateman: 29, 35, 62, 63, 75, 85, 86, 89, 105, 106, 108, 123, 128 • Stockfood / Jean Cazals: 130 • Stockfood / Frank Wieder: 131 • The Image Bank: 9, 17, 81, 98, 99, 124

PRECEDING PAGE
A shepherdess watches over her flock on the Altiplano.

Editorial Director (U.S.): Michelle Bisson
Editors: Deborah Grahame, Mabelle Yeo, Crystal Ouyang
Copyreader: Daphne Hougham
Designers: Jailani Basari, Sean Lee
Cover picture researcher: Connie Gardner
Picture researchers: Thomas Khoo, Joshua Ang

Marshall Cavendish Benchmark
99 White Plains Road
Tarrytown, NY 10591
Web site: www.marshallcavendish.us

All Internet sites were correct and accurate at the time of printing. All monetary figures in this publication are in U.S. dollars.

Library of Congress Cataloging-in-Publication Data
Pateman, Robert, 1954–
   Bolivia / by Robert Pateman & Marcus Cramer.
      p. cm. — (Cultures of the world (2nd ed.)
   Summary: "Provides comprehensive information on the geography, history, governmental structure, economy, cultural
      diversity, peoples, religion, and culture of Bolivia" — Provided by publisher.
   Includes bibliographical references and index.
      ISBN-13: 978-0-7614-2066-8
      ISBN-10: 0-7614-2066-5
   1.   Bolivia—Juvenile literature.   I. Cramer, Marcus. II. Title. III. Series.
   F3308.5.P37 1996
   984—dc22   2006002425

Printed in China

987654321

CONTENTS

Bolivian children on their way to school.

Men do the knitting on Taquile Island in Lake Titicaca.

INTRODUCTION

THE REPUBLIC OF BOLIVIA, a landlocked country in the heart of the South American continent, was once at the center of the Spanish colonial empire. Bolivia's poverty dramatically contrasts with the wealth of its geography, biodiversity, natural resources, and cultures.

The country has vast snowcapped mountain ranges, deep gorges, fertile valleys, and a steamy jungle region that serves as the gateway to the Amazon. Enormous mineral wealth has dominated the country's history. Ancient Incan civilization and the Spanish colonial rule have combined to produce a rich cultural heritage. Ancestral gods persist within the rituals of modern Roman Catholicism. Spanish festivals also incorporate ancient Incan customs. A tradition of lively dance, haunting music, and colorful weaving keeps old traditions alive.

Although Bolivia's ancient traditions and ways of life struggle to survive in a rapidly changing and sometimes hostile global environment, its people remain hopeful of a better future.

GEOGRAPHY

BOLIVIA IS NOT A LARGE COUNTRY compared with its South American neighbors, but it still covers 424,164 square miles (1,098,580 square km), making it twice as big as Texas and only a little smaller than Alaska. It is a landlocked country with no direct access to the sea.

Bolivia shares borders with Peru and Chile to the west, Argentina to the south, Paraguay to the southeast, and Brazil to the east and north. Most of the population lives on the High Plateau, or Altiplano (ahl-tee-PLAH-noh), between two chains of the Andes Mountains. Most people would consider this region to be "typically Bolivian." However, the country also has large areas of tropical rain forest, savanna, swamp, and semidesert.

Bolivia has rich resources of oil and minerals, and in the past much of the nation's wealth came from silver and tin mining. Bolivia's considerable natural gas resources, mostly foreign-owned, have been nationalized by President Evo Morales, thus returning them to Bolivian control.

Left: **The spectacular cliffs on the Island of the Moon, one of the largest islands in Lake Titicaca.**

Opposite: **The Island of the Sun overlooks the clear blue waters of Lake Titicaca.**

THE DIFFERENT REGIONS

Bolivia has three main regions: the Altiplano or High Plateau, the valleys, and the lowlands.

The Altiplano is one of the highest inhabited areas in the world. This plateau lies between two ranges of the Andes Mountains at an average height of 12,000 feet (3,600 m). It is a high, bleak, windswept, cold, and barren region. Parts of the Altiplano are vast areas of solitude, while other parts, especially around the city of La Paz, are more densely populated than any other region of Bolivia.

The valleys include the Yungas (deep valleys and high ridges on the eastern slopes of the Andes) and cities such as Cochabamba, Sucre, and Tarija are located in the wider valleys. The Yungas are noted for their rugged terrain; hills and gorges tangle into each other, making many areas almost inaccessible. Although some valleys are narrow, others fan out into well-watered, fertile basins. This land is more fertile and more hospitable than the Altiplano, with a milder climate. Thirty percent of the population of Bolivia lives in the valleys, which contain 40 percent of the country's cultivated land.

The lowlands, which lie to the north and east and stretch to Brazil and Paraguay, make up about two-thirds of Bolivia. The area around Trinidad is covered with rich tropical forests, part of the Amazon River basin. Other areas are open savannas or swamps. In the south the lowlands become the South Bolivian Chaco, part of the Gran Chaco. For seven to eight months this is a semidesert, but it turns into a swamp when the rains arrive. This is one of the hottest parts of South America during the rainy season, when temperatures of 100°F (37.8°C) are common. The Chaco is sparsely populated, as are the lowlands generally. Few countries in the world are blessed with such geographic diversity.

Despite its name, which means "swampy plain," Cochabamba is one of Bolivia's most pleasant cities, with a climate similar to Mediterranean Europe. It is surrounded by rich farmland, which has earned the region the title of "breadbasket of Bolivia."

THE LEGEND OF ILLIMANI

Bolivian indigenous culture has many wonderful legends. According to the legend of Mount Illimani, two mountains once stood above the place where the city of La Paz now stands. The god who created them could never decide which he loved the most. Both looked different in different light, and he was always walking across the canyon floor to see them at their best.

The god was watching Mount Illimani one day when he decided it really was his favorite. Using his sling, he hurled a giant boulder at the other peak, and the mountaintop rolled far away. The god cried, "*Sajama*!" which means "Go away!" The mountain is still called by that name. The lower half of the mountain in its original place to this day is called Mururata, which means "beheaded."

The La Paz fire brigade is seldom called on to put out fires because it is so difficult for flames to spread with the low oxygen density found at such high altitude. However, during the rainy season, floods keep the fire brigade very busy.

MOUNTAINS

The Andes Mountains run the entire length of South America, from the northern coast of the Caribbean Sea to Tierra del Fuego at the southern end of Chile, a distance of 5,500 miles (8,850 km). Before they enter Bolivia, the Andes divide into two ranges. The Cordillera Occidental runs through the west of the country and forms Bolivia's border with Chile. There are several active volcanoes in this range, and they occasionally give off gases. The highest point is Mount Sajama at 21,463 feet (6,542 m).

The Cordillera Oriental passes to the east and reaches its most impressive section, called Cordillera Real, around La Paz, where there is a towering line of snowcapped peaks. The most famous of these is Mount Illimani at 21,200 feet (6,462 m). This extraordinary mountain range has more than 600 peaks that are higher than 16,400 feet (5,000 m).

Farther south the Andes rejoin and widen. This forms the area known as the Puna. The Andes are rich in mineral deposits, including zinc, tin, and silver.

A mountainous land-scape. Four mountain peaks on western Bolivia rank among the highest in the world.

RIVERS, SWAMPS, AND LAKES

Bolivia has three drainage systems: the Amazon system in the northwest, north, and northeast; the Lake Titicaca system in the Altiplano; and a third that carries water southwest toward Argentina.

The Beni and Mamoré rivers collect much of the water that flows east from the Andes and form headwaters of the Amazon River. Many rivers on the plains are deep enough to take shallow draft boats and barges and are important for transportation in an area where there are few roads. It is not possible to travel along the rivers to the Amazon proper and the sea beyond because of rapids.

Because of its vast size and the bitter cold, the Uyuni Salt Flat has been called the Alaska of Bolivia.

A second drainage system starts on the Altiplano with hundreds of streams flowing down from the snow line into Lake Titicaca. The Desaguadero River flows south from Titicaca into Lake Poopó, a shallow, salty body of water rarely more than 10 feet (3 m) deep. It usually covers 1,000 square miles (2,500 square km), but after a heavy rain the lake can expand to the edge of Oruro, 30 miles (45 km) away.

The Lacajahuira River flows south from Poopó and empties into the Coipasa Salt Field. This is a wide, marshy, salt-encrusted wilderness with one small body of water at its lowest point. The magnificently desolate Uyuni Salt Flat lies farther south and is even bigger, covering 4,085 square miles (10,580 square km).

The third drainage system is made up of water that runs off the Yungas and flows south into the Pilcomayo River and its tributaries. These run southeast to join the Paraguay and the Plate rivers.

CLIMATE

Because Bolivia is situated in the southern hemisphere, its summer and winter are the reverse of what they are in the northern hemisphere. Summer brings the most rain. Winter is generally drier and more pleasant, with day after day of clear blue skies. The higher areas get cold, and between June and August the fierce *surazo* (soo-RAH-zoh) winds blow in from the Argentine pampas, bringing storms and severe drops in temperature to the normally hot eastern lowlands.

The eastern slopes of the Andes mountain ranges below 6,000 feet (1,829 m) have a tropical climate. Average rainfall is 30–50 inches (76–127 cm) and neither temperature nor rainfall varies much. The Yungas, 6,000–9,500 feet (1,829–2,896 m), are seldom cold. This area has the most pleasant climate, often described as permanent spring. The Altiplano zone is always cool. Summer brings thunderstorms and winter occasional snow. Above 13,000 feet (3,962 m) there are arctic conditions.

Century plants grow at 13,000 feet (3,900 m) and flower every 80 to 100 years.

FLORA AND FAUNA

Bolivia's vegetation is as varied as its climate. On the Altiplano only hardy plants survive. *Ichu*, a coarse bunched grass, is the most common vegetation and is the basic food of the llama. *Thola*, a wind-resistant shrub, also grows here, as do cacti. Along the banks of Lake Titicaca *totora* reeds are abundant. Native *quishuara* and *khena* trees grow on the Altiplano, and eucalyptus and pine trees have been introduced around the lake.

The Yungas have a wide range of natural trees, including cedar, mahogany, and walnut. One of the most useful is the *cinchona*, from which the malaria-fighting drug quinine was first extracted.

In the lowland plains the Bolivian rain forest contains hundreds of species of trees, many of which grow to enormous heights. An equally diverse range of plants grows under the forest canopy.

The northern and central lowlands consist of grassy savannas and isolated woodlands, but farther south in the Chaco, little survives the fierce conditions except cacti and scorched grasses.

Bolivia's wildlife is equally varied. The llama, alpaca, guanaco, and vicuña, all native to the Andes, live in the highlands. The llama and alpaca are domesticated versions of the guanaco. The vicuña is not kept domestically, but it is heavily hunted for its silky wool.

The Altiplano is also home to several species of rodents, including the cavy, a guinea pig bred for its meat and often kept as a pet.

Lake Titicaca is home to many different species of birds, including gulls, ducks, geese, and hummingbirds. Lake Poopó to the south is famous for its once endangered flamingos.

The swamps and plains of the lowlands have a very different ecosystem. Here are anteaters; wild pigs called peccaries; pumas; marsh deer; and the capybara, the world's largest rodent. The rivers and swamps also support countless numbers of fish, frogs, butterflies, toads, and lizards. The most remarkable bird of the region is the rhea, a large, flightless bird similar to an ostrich.

Many of these animals are hunted for food. The armadillo is considered a delicacy, and its shell can be used to make musical instruments. The only reason wildlife has survived so well is that the region has remained sparsely populated until now.

The Incas had a special respect for the puma. According to Bolivian folklore, when some of the moon disappears, it means that the puma has crept up and taken a bite out of it.

LAKE TITICACA

Lake Titicaca is remarkable because of its size, its altitude, and its great beauty. It is the second-largest lake in South America, covering 3,200 square miles (8,288 square km), and it has 41 islands. It is impossible to see the northwestern shore from the lakeside town of Copacabana. Its beauty comes from a combination of its deep color, the reflection of the blue sky, and in the south, the backdrop of mountain peaks.

In fact, Titicaca is almost two lakes; the smaller southern body of water is joined to the main lake only by a narrow strait. The border between Peru and Bolivia goes through the center of the lake, which means that traffic from La Paz has to cross the strait by ferry, rather than take the western shoreline route that would cross the Peruvian border. While buses and cars go across on small platform rafts, passengers transfer to little speedboats, which are tossed around by waves if there is any wind.

Titicaca lies at an altitude of 12,500 feet (3,810 m) and is the highest navigable body of water in the world. It is also an exceptionally deep lake, reaching depths of about 900 feet (274 m).

The lake played an important role in the religious beliefs of the early civilizations of the area. The Incas believed this was the spot where humankind was created. Rumors still persist that Lake Titicaca holds great hidden treasures. According to some accounts, the Incas threw vast amounts of gold and silver into the lake to prevent it from being stolen by the Spanish. Other legends tell of ancient cities hidden beneath the deep waters of the lake.

The most diverse wildlife of all is concentrated in Bolivia's tropical forests. Mammals include monkeys, anteaters, tapirs, jaguars, and the spectacled bear. The rivers are alive with fish, including the meat-eating piranha, and there are hundreds of species of birds and thousands of species of insects.

Bolivia's environment is facing new problems as roads are constructed to open up previously inaccessible areas, threatening Bolivia's wildlife.

THE DISPUTED CAPITALS

Sucre was the capital at Bolivia's independence and is still the judicial capital of Bolivia, but legislative and executive functions are located in La Paz. La Paz is the second biggest city in Bolivia, with a population rising toward the 1 million mark. About half of the population is of native birth. La Paz was founded in October 1548 by Alonso de Mendoza. The Spaniards hoped to find gold here but were disappointed. Instead, La Paz survived because of its position on the trade route between Potosí and Lima, Peru. It is the political and commercial center of the nation.

Sucre lies southeast of La Paz. It has not grown as large as La Paz, but most people from Sucre believe their city is more beautiful, and it certainly has a milder, more pleasant climate. Founded in 1539, Sucre is still the most Spanish-looking of Bolivia's cities, with many old colonial buildings with white facades and orange tile roofs.

Recently Santa Cruz has become the largest city in Bolivia, as well as the industrial center of the country. Santa Cruz has considerable economic influence and is currently competing with La Paz in the realm of political dominance.

At 11,900 feet (3,627 m), La Paz is the highest city of its size in the world. The air is thin enough to cause some discomfort in breathing until one adjusts to the new conditions.

Altitude has more influence on the climate of Bolivia than the seasons do. A visitor can experience a change in climate just by walking up or down a thousand feet or so on a Bolivian footpath.

HISTORY

THE HEARTLAND OF BOLIVIA consists of a vast area of arable land high up in the Andes Mountains on the great Altiplano, or High Plateau. The first people to inhabit this region were probably nomadic hunters who crossed the Bering Strait from Siberia and moved southward through the Americas.

By 1400 B.C. they were established on the Altiplano, where they became farmers. Around this time a new art style arose. Called Chavín, it was far more advanced than anything that had been produced previously in the Americas.

Sometime between A.D. 500 and A.D. 800 there emerged an even more advanced culture called Tiahuanaco, which was to influence people as far away as Ecuador. Farmers developed advanced methods of irrigation, and it was probably at this time that the potato was first cultivated.

Above: **Carved faces on the wall of a temple at Tiahuanaco. The masonry at Tiahuanaco exhibits the earliest use of metal to hold stones together.**

Opposite: **The Tiahuanaco and Inca civilizations left behind many ruins. This is a Ponce monolith in the Kalasasaya.**

The political and religious center of this civilization is believed to have been at Tiahuanaco, on the shores of Lake Titicaca, although there was an equally impressive sister city at Huari, in what is now Peru. The ruins at Tiahuanaco show that these people had developed the technology to convey enormous blocks of building stone across the lake.

At its height Tiahuanaco had a population of around 20,000 people, but after 300 or 400 years it fell into decline. Nobody is sure why this happened. It might have been due to war, or perhaps to one of the extended drought periods that has affected the area in cyclical climate changes.

TIAHUANACO

The archaeological site of Tiahuanaco lies less than two hours' drive from La Paz. It is not, at first glance, a particularly impressive site because much of the stone has been carried away over the years to build churches and bridges.

There remain the mound of the Akapana, a great step pyramid, and the Kalasasaya (*above*), a great sunken temple. Just visible through the archway is the large sculpted figure that stands outside the Kalasasaya. Other sculptures include several freestanding statues, two carved doorways, and some stone faces in the walls of the sunken temple.

For archaeologists Tiahuanaco is an exciting center that continues to produce surprises. Excavations in this century have revealed that the site was not just an isolated ceremonial center, as first thought, but a bustling metropolis that was home to thousands of people.

Scientists have discovered evidence of a system of raised fields, which both protected the crops from the waters of Lake Titicaca and retained heat during the cold Altiplano nights. The center of the pyramid has yet to be fully explored.

In 2000 the site of Tiahuanaco was added to the United Nations Educational, Scientific and Cultural Organization (UNESCO) World Heritage List. The World Heritage List forms the framework for international cooperation in preserving and protecting cultural treasures and natural areas throughout the world.

THE INCAS

The decline of the Tiahuanaco empire left a power vacuum that was eventually filled by the dramatic rise of the Incan Empire.

The Incas originally came from the Cuzco Valley in Peru, but from around A.D. 1400 they expanded to build an empire that stretched for 2,000 miles (3,220 km) and probably had, according to various specialists' estimates, between 5 to 12 million subjects. To gain more control over the resistant Aymará people, the Incas moved many speakers of their own language into the region.

An Incan wall still standing. From their capital in Cuzco, Peru, the Incas conquered a large territory and exported their technology and culture throughout the region.

The Incas were magnificent organizers and engineers. They constructed great cities linked by stone roads and established a system of runners to carry messages between cities. They built suspension bridges across wide gorges and terraced the mountainsides to grow crops.

Incan artists worked in ceramics, silver, and gold. Their weavers produced magnificent textiles. These were so fine that the Spanish mistook Incan cotton for silk. Incan culture was rich in music and dance and had wonderful legends and folktales that were passed on by word of mouth. Many are still told today.

The Incas neither used the wheel nor developed a system of writing. The Incan Empire left two major legacies: the ruins of their great cities and a language, Quechua, that continues to be spoken throughout much of South America. The Incan Empire lasted about a hundred years before the Spanish conquered it. Whether Incan culture was already in decline by then is debatable, but the Incas were certainly no match for the better-armed invaders who reached the borders of their empire in 1532.

FRANCISCO PISARRO

An early engraving of Pizarro. Many Spaniards who came to Bolivia were searching for El Dorado, the legendary city so rich that the streets were paved with gold.

ARRIVAL OF THE SPANISH

In 1492 Columbus became the first European since the Vikings to sail to the American continents. Pope Alexander VI decreed that this "pagan" land should be divided between Portugal and Spain. Inspired by the pope's message, adventurers and soldiers set off to seek their fortunes in the New World.

In 1532 Francisco Pizarro and Diego de Almagro, two Spanish adventurers, arrived at the Incan capital with just 170 soldiers. They found an empire facing serious political problems. The sudden death of the Lord Inca had left the leadership of the empire in doubt, and a civil war had broken out between two sons of the Inca, Huáscar and Atahualpa.

According to some Spanish chroniclers of the period, the Incan nobility was amazed by these strange, white-skinned, bearded men who rode on horses as if joined to the animals. The Incas, as shown in these chronicles, had presumed that the conquistadores had been sent by the gods to settle the turmoil in the empire. As such, the Spaniards met little resistance.

The Spaniards arranged a meeting with the victorious Atahualpa and imprisoned him. Although the Incas paid a huge ransom in gold and silver to get their leader back, the Spanish executed him and took over the empire.

Within two years much of Incan society had been destroyed, and Pizarro and Almagro had divided South America between themselves. What is now Bolivia was ruled by Almagro and became known as Upper Peru or Charcas. Almagro's new wealth did him little good; he was assassinated by fellow Spaniards in 1538.

SILVER

In 1544 Diego Huallpa, a native herder, lost some llamas. Unable to find them he set up camp and lit a fire to keep warm. To his surprise the earth beneath his fire started to flow in a stream of molten metal. Huallpa had discovered silver. This subsequently brought thousands of settlers to South America. By 1650 the town of Potosí had a population of 160,000 and was one of the greatest cities in the Americas. The silver mined at Potosí was taken to the coast on the backs of llamas. From there Spanish galleons ferried it across the Atlantic to Europe.

For 200 years the silver mines of Potosí (*right*) paid the Spanish empire's bills. According to local folklore, the Spanish took enough silver to build a bridge all the way to Spain.

The miners descended into the shafts by ropes, worked 12-hour shifts by candlelight, and were kept underground for days or weeks. Thousands died each year from disease, ill treatment, and accidents. Most of the work was done by indigenous peoples brought in from all over the Andes. African slaves were imported, but few survived the cold. The mines were so feared that mothers deliberately crippled their sons so they would not be conscripted. It was at this time that the Spanish began to encourage the miners to chew coca leaves (the source of cocaine) to help them endure the wretched conditions. Coca had previously been reserved for Incan priests and royalty.

La Paz was founded in 1548 as a staging point between the mines and the sea and soon became a major city. Oruro was the site of a second major silver find. Upper Peru, as Bolivia was then called, was soon one of the wealthiest corners of the Spanish empire, and in 1559 a local government, the Audiencia of Charcas, was established under the control of the viceroy of Peru. The government was based in Chuquisaca, which became the political and educational center of the colony.

Many of the Spanish who came to South America turned to farming and became the new landowning aristocracy. Because the Spaniards took the best land, the indigenous peoples were pushed back to the higher mountain slopes, where they lived as tenant farmers, forced to supply the new owners with food and labor.

Plaza Murillo in La Paz was named after the rebel president Pedro Murillo. Murillo was captured and executed on January 26, 1813.

SPAIN DECLINES

The 1770s were a troubled time. After years of mistreatment, the indigenous population rebelled. The most notable of these revolts was led by Tupac Katari and his wife, Bartolina Sisa, and included a great siege against La Paz from the highland above.

The rebels were eventually captured and executed. Then there was an economic crisis. Between 1803 and 1825 silver production fell by 80 percent. By 1846, 10,000 mines had been abandoned.

In Upper Peru unrest was growing among the Creoles (people of Spanish parents born in South America). Having played a major part in building Spain's American empire, they were angry that top government positions were reserved for only those born in Spain.

Napoleon Bonaparte's conquest of Spain gave the colonies the perfect opportunity to rebel. In 1809 Creoles in Chuquisaca and La Paz declared that they would recognize the exiled Spanish king but not the governors sent by the French.

On July 16, rebels in La Paz imprisoned the governor and elected Pedro Domingo Murillo president. The Spanish viceroy in Lima sent an army and quickly crushed the revolution.

Some of the rebels fled to the hills and carried out a guerrilla campaign that lasted 16 years. Ironically, Upper Peru, which had started the revolution in South America, was the last colony to gain its freedom.

THE FIGHT FOR FREEDOM

In 1814 in Europe, Napoleon was defeated and the Spanish monarchy restored, but South America had cultivated a taste for freedom, and the fight went on.

Simón Bolívar was a leading figure in this struggle. In a series of brilliant military campaigns, he brought independence to Venezuela, Colombia, and Ecuador. In 1824 he sent his revolutionary army to liberate Peru and bring colonial rule in South America to an end. Marshal Antonio José de Sucre was in charge of the campaign and won victories at Junín on August 6 and at Ayacucho on December 9 of the same year.

Historically, Upper Peru had always been linked with Lima, but that city had only just been freed from Spanish rule and there was no government in place. Many of the officers who had supported Sucre, particularly those who had deserted from the royalist army, wanted Upper Peru to be independent. Bolívar himself was against the idea and wanted the decision to wait until a new congress was formed in Lima. However, in February 1825, Sucre declared that Upper Peru must decide its own future, and on August 6, exactly a year after the first decisive battle, Upper Peru became an independent country, with Sucre as its first president.

Shortly afterward the new nation adopted the name Bolivia in honor of the great freedom fighter, and the city of Chuquisaca, where independence had been declared, became known as Sucre.

A monument to Antonio José de Sucre in La Paz. Sucre was called "the Immaculate" for his high moral qualities. He was assassinated in 1830 while he was on his way home to Ecuador to retire.

BOLÍVAR—THE GREAT FREEDOM FIGHTER

Simón Bolívar was born in Caracas, Venezuela, in 1783. His father died when Bolívar was 3, and his mother died six years later. As was usual for young men from upper-class South American families, he was sent to Spain to complete his education. He married the daughter of a Spanish nobleman and brought her back to South America. She died of yellow fever only a few months after arriving in her new home.

Bolívar visited Europe again in 1804. During his time there he was inspired by the works of thinkers and writers such as Voltaire, among others. It was then that the idea of an independent South America took hold of his imagination.

He returned to his homeland and joined the growing independence movement, which in 1810 expelled the Spanish governor from Caracas. Bolívar was sent to London, where he tried unsuccessfully to win British support for the struggle. He sailed back to South America, but when the revolution was crushed by troops loyal to Spain, he had to flee the country. While in exile he wrote his most important political work, *El Manifesto de Cartagena* (*The Cartegena Manifesto*).

In 1819 Bolívar marched his army across the snow-covered Andes and took the Spanish army by surprise. He won a series of brilliant military victories and became president of the newly independent nation of Gran Colombia (roughly covering present-day Colombia, Panama, Venezuela, and Ecuador). In 1824 his army, under the command of Antonio José de Sucre, crushed the last Spanish royalists in Ecuador and Peru.

Bolívar had the vision of uniting all of South America into one great nation and was disillusioned when the continent broke up into a collection of independent countries. He became unpopular as a leader and was nearly assassinated. He resigned as president and died in 1830, at the age of 47, worn out from a lifetime of fighting. Nevertheless, to many South Americans he will always be the legendary *El Libertador*.

DISASTROUS WARS

Although the individual South American nations had gained their independence, their borders were not clearly defined. As a result Bolivia was dragged into a series of disastrous wars that resulted in the loss of large parts of its territory.

The first blow came 60 years after independence. Bolivia owned land on the coast that was rich with nitrates and guano (bird droppings used for fertilizer), but Bolivia was not in a position to exploit these resources. Instead, Bolivia gave Chile permission to develop them. A dispute developed over what taxes the Chileans should pay for this concession, and this led to war in 1879, in which British fertilizer companies had a hidden hand.

Even though Peru came to Bolivia's aid, the Bolivian army was crushed at the Battle of Tacna. Bolivia played little part in the rest of the War of the Pacific and watched while Chile devastated Peru and took over a large part of Bolivian territory, including its access to the sea. Even today Bolivia's relationship with Chile is shadowed by the question of sea access.

The war discredited Bolivia's military leaders, and this allowed the rich mine owners to gain power. Around this time mining started to recover from its earlier slump. The price of silver rose, and production increased as a result of investment in new equipment. In addition, industrialization in the West created a demand for tin, of which Bolivia had vast reserves.

A series of wars with neighboring countries resulted in a large loss of land for Bolivia.

THE CHACO WAR

Bolivia had a liberal government from 1899 to 1920 and enjoyed one of the calmest periods in its history. World War I in Europe brought new demands for tin, but although demand was high, the price remained low.

In 1932 a border dispute with Paraguay developed. The two nations are separated by the Gran Chaco, a desert plain that no one had been concerned about. By the 1930s there were rumors of oil in the region, and the two nations started to argue over the position of the border. Bolivia set up a fort in the Chaco, which the Paraguayan army seized. Negotiations were taking place when the troops on the ground started fighting. The conflict escalated rapidly.

Two oil companies, hoping to win rights to develop whatever oil was found, provided funds to cover the cost of the war: one backed Bolivia, while the other sided with Paraguay. Having just lost a war, Paraguay saw this as an opportunity to restore national pride.

The war lasted three years and ended in defeat for Bolivia. As many as 100,000 Bolivians were either killed, wounded, or captured. At the end Bolivia had lost another large part of her territory. Ironically no oil was ever discovered in the disputed territory.

Veterans of the Chaco War. The war brought major changes to Bolivian society. Mestizos and Europeans had fought side by side, breaking down racial barriers and increasing the common feeling of dissatisfaction. The war inspired the Chaco generation to change the way Bolivia was run. Some put their energy into art and literature, and others formed new political parties.

MODERN HISTORY

For many indigenous Bolivians who fought in the war, it was their first taste of being part of a nation as opposed to just being part of a local community. Thanks to the political conscience they gained, many participated in social movements in the years following the Chaco War. Several new political parties were formed, the most important of which was the Movimiento Nacionalista Revolucionario (MNR). The MNR drew support from mine workers and peasants to win the 1951 election.

Víctor Paz Estenssoro became president and introduced a range of reforms. Mines were nationalized, the indigenous population was given the right to vote, land laws were reformed, and primary education was introduced into the villages. The MNR remained in power for 12 years before losing popularity due to their failure to improve the standard of living for the general population.

In 1964 there was a military coup. This marked the start of another period of instability, with one military government replacing another. At the worst times, particularly during the late 1970s, presidents resorted to imprisoning and torturing their opponents. Dictators especially known for such practices were Generals Hugo Bánzer Suárez and Luis García Meza.

Democracy was reestablished in 1982, at a moment when Latin America was entering an economic crisis. In 1985 Víctor Paz Estenssoro became president for the third time. He introduced some harsh economic reforms but managed to make both the political and economic situation more stable. During the 1990s successive governments opened up Bolivia's market, paving the way for massive privatizations as part of a general strategy coordinated with international institutions to develop the economy and repay the country's enormous debt.

Failure to improve the living conditions for many Bolivians, as well as the dismantling of many social services, the controversy over coca policies, and the selling off of natural resources led to social conflicts, street protests, and ultimately a profound political crisis.

At the center of the conflict were indigenous organizations demanding social and economic rights. After the toppling of two presidents, elections were called for in 2005, leading to the victory of Socialist Evo Morales-Ayma, a former coca farmer as well as the first indigenous man ever to become president of Bolivia. It remains to be seen if the political situation will stabilize with the new government as it attempts to satisfy diverse and sometimes conflicting interests.

In 1967 the Marxist hero Che Guevara, who had been training guerrillas in southern Bolivia, was captured and killed by the Bolivian army.

GOVERNMENT

BOLIVIA IS A REPUBLIC with the president as head of state. Presidents are elected for five-year terms, and they select a cabinet of ministers to help them run the country. Presidents have the right to rule by decree.

At election time presidential candidates nominate a running mate and they campaign together. Elections are highly charged affairs, with aggressive campaigning. The national television station gives all candidates equal air time, but parties can buy additional time on other stations. Generally, people have been cynical about elections, unsure of how fair they will be.

When there is no clear electoral majority, which is usually the case, parliament has the final say. This means weeks of bargaining behind closed doors. For example, in 1989 Gonzálo Sánchez de Lozada won the most votes but did not have enough support to form a majority. The second-place candidate, General Hugo Bánzer Suárez, gave his support to Jaime Paz Zamora, who had finished third. This surprised most people because the two men had been adversaries. As a result, Paz Zamora gained a majority and became the country's president.

The president often wields power beyond the parameters of his office when his coalition has a majority in parliament. In the past the military often removed governments by force. Strikes by labor unions have also influenced the direction of the country. A vast army of bureaucrats sometimes makes governing a slow and frustrating experience.

In December 2005 a presidential election was won by an absolute majority making backroom bargaining between political parties unnecessary. The president elect, Evo Morales, himself of indigenous origin, has vowed to preside over a constituent assembly to establish a new constitution.

Above: **Every village in Bolivia has a memorial to the Chaco War in which 10,000 Bolivians lost their lives. The Chaco War was as traumatic to Bolivia as the Vietnam War was to the United States, and caused the whole nation to lose faith in itself.**

Opposite: **A military parade in La Paz. The military has played a large role in Bolivian politics.**

Government offices in La Paz.

CONGRESS

Bolivia's national congress, or Congreso Nacional, consists of two houses: a chamber of deputies and a chamber of senators. Congress generally meets for a 90-day session.

Each of the country's departments has an allocation of seats in congress according to its population. Until 1952 only literate people could vote. This was one method the aristocracy used to retain power. Since 1952 all married Bolivians over the age of 18 and all singles over 21 have the right to vote.

The chamber of deputies consists of 130 members elected for five-year terms. The chamber of senators is made up of 27 senators, three from each department, elected for five years. The vice president is the presiding officer of the chamber of senators. The role of the chamber of senators is to review and approve the work of the chamber of deputies.

The third branch of authority is the judiciary. The supreme court is based in Sucre and consists of 12 judges selected by congress. Judges serve 10-year terms on the supreme court.

This system of government is similar to that in the United States. Bolivia, like the United States, has a constitution that lays down basic freedoms and rules for government. Prior to the reinstallment of democracy in 1982, the Bolivian constitution had often been ignored or suspended by politicians, with the military frequently overriding the constitutional process.

THE AYNI SYSTEM

On the Altiplano most decisions are still made at village level by the *ayni* (AYE-nee), a political, economic, and social system that has been in place at least since Incan times. Under the *ayni* system the men of the village meet to discuss what needs to be done. Once a decision is made, everyone works together on the project for the good of the community.

The *jilakata* (HEE-lah-kah-ta), or chief, has a particularly important role to play. After listening to a discussion, he makes the final decision. Generally the chief is selected based on age, but factors such as personality and community support are also important. Acts of God also help. The Altiplano often has lightning storms, and anyone who survives being hit by lightning wins awe and prestige.

The *ayni* system also works in a less formal way. At a wedding all the villagers bring gifts, perhaps sheep or beer. This helps the family afford the expensive celebration. However, the *ayni* system demands that one gives back twice as much as one received. For example, if someone brought four sheep to your son's wedding, you have to give eight back when there is a wedding in their family!

LOCAL GOVERNMENT AND AUTONOMY

Bolivia is divided into nine departments, each ruled by a prefect until recently appointed by the president. During the 2005 elections prefects were elected by popular vote for the first time. The departments are subdivided into provinces, which are controlled by subprefects. Provinces are divided into cantons. Important cities each have their own elected council led by an elected mayor.

Although local governments do much of the administration, important decisions are usually made by the central government. In addition, by keeping control over many key appointments, the president can impose authority over the whole system.

As presidents do not appoint people who are likely to oppose them, politicians who want to further their political careers know they can do so only with the president's support. However, much of this is changing, with emphasis placed on regional autonomy.

During the 1990s a system of local enfranchisement called Participacíon Popular (Popular Participation) was established under Gonzálo Sánchez de Lozada, and the first steps toward a more independent region and autonomy of indigenous communities were discussed publicly.

There is a new consensus among all major political forces that administration should be decentralized. With such ideas in the air, many leaders of the department of Santa Cruz have argued for their own autonomy.

General Luis García Meza came to power in a 1980 military coup. For 14 months he suppressed all opposition by imprisoning, torturing, and murdering opponents. When Meza was finally ousted, the Bolivian economy was deep in debt. Although Meza fled to Brazil, he was tried in absentia for his crimes by the supreme court in April 1994 and sentenced to 30 years in jail. A year later Meza was extradited from Brazil to Bolivia and began serving his prison sentence.

POLITICS BY FORCE

Bolivian politics was once violent and unpredictable, with few presidents finishing a full term. On many occasions the army had nullified elections and seized power. In 1980 the country recorded its 189th coup in 155 years of independence.

As a result, Bolivia has had some brazen and ruthless heads of state, many of whom became increasingly authoritarian and dictatorial while in office, ignoring the constitution and suppressing human rights.

One of the worst was President Mariano Melgarejo, who was in power from 1864 to 1871. During his years in office he diverted vast amounts of the nation's wealth into his own pockets. He seized land from the indigenous people and conceded large areas of northern Bolivia to Brazil. In an incident that is still shrouded in mystery, it is suspected that Melgarejo either himself shot and killed a former president who was conspiring against him or was in the room when his officers carried out the murder.

Bolivia has also produced some highly respected presidents, including Antonio José de Sucre, founder of the country and its first president (1826–28); Andrés de Santa Cruz (1829–39), a powerful and influential figure known as the Napoleon of the Andes; and Ismael Montes, who served two terms in office, from 1904 to 1908 and from 1913 to 1917. Montes was one of the first politicians to be concerned about the rights of the indigenous community.

Víctor Paz Estenssoro, leader of the MNR, served several terms in power. He implemented many reforms after the 1952 revolution and proved himself willing to make unpopular decisions to stop runaway inflation.

At the moment the Bolivian democracy is enjoying a remarkably profound evolution and has hopefully entered an era of new political dynamism. The early half of the first decade of the 21st century has been marked by intense social movements with over 100 deaths caused by repression during the second presidency of Gonzálo Sánchez de Lozada. In the wake of a 2003 massacre, public opinion turned against Sánchez de Lozada, forcing him to resign and flee the country. Sánchez de Lozada's vice president, journalist Carlos Mesa, took office in a divided country, promising to satisfy indigenous demands for a reconsideration of how to manage Bolivia's rich natural resources. Mesa also promised there would be no repression under his interim government, a promise that he made good on.

In 2005 Mesa, too, resigned after failing to bridge the hopeless gap between the goals of foreign gas companies and Bolivia's impoverished indigenous majority. This resignation set in motion a complicated process that led to the election of Evo Morales, who, in 2006, initiated plans to nationalize the natural gas fields.

Evo Morales, leader of the strongest indigenous party in the nation, Movement Toward Socialism (MAS), won the Bolivian presidency in a landslide election in 2005.

Only one Bolivian woman has ever served as president. Lidia Gueiler Téjada was interim president from November 1979 to July 1980.

Víctor Paz Estenssoro in 1985. His 1952 government assumed control over the tin mines and granted the indigenous people full civil rights.

THE 1952 REVOLUTION

The revolution of 1952 was the single most dramatic event in 20th-century Bolivian politics. It started a chain of events that still affects the country.

By the 1950s most Bolivians were unhappy about conditions in their country; the majority of people were living in poverty, while a small elite enjoyed most of the wealth and political power.

The newly formed MNR promised to reform this situation and won widespread support among the peasants and miners.

Under the skillful leadership of Víctor Paz Estenssoro, the MNR won the 1951 election, only to have power snatched away from it in a military coup. On this occasion, however, the mood in the nation was different. A popular revolution broke out and after several pitched battles, each more violent than before, the army was crushed and Estenssoro's civilian government was placed in power in 1952.

The revolutionary government immediately nationalized the already declining mining industry and started a series of economic and educational projects. More importantly, in August 1953 the government implemented one of the most far-reaching land reform acts of the century, giving indigenous farmers ownership of any land they farmed. The new government also broke the absolute power of the small ruling elite by giving every adult Bolivian citizen the right to vote. Previously, the franchise had been extended only to the literate.

FLAG AND EMBLEM

The Bolivian flag is divided into three horizontal stripes of red, gold, and green. The flag flown on government buildings also includes the Bolivian coat of arms in the center of the gold band. The red band in the flag represents both animals and the armed forces, the green is for fertility and the land, and the yellow stands for the nation's mineral wealth.

The national emblem (*right*) includes a condor, Mount Potosí, and a woolly alpaca.

The Bolivian national anthem is the "National Hymn of Bolivia."

FOREIGN POLICY

The desire for access to the sea is evident in Bolivian foreign policy. Every time a political party starts to become unpopular, it brings up this issue. There seems no possibility of Chile conceding land to Bolivia, and this appears likely to remain a thorn between the nations for years to come.

Bolivia has a strong relationship with Argentina, a major trading partner, and many Bolivians work there. In 1992 Bolivia developed closer trading ties with its neighbors by officially joining the Andean Free-Trade Area, which, among other things, removes trade barriers between members. However, Bolivians have become increasingly reluctant about joining free-trade area agreements with the United States, fearing unfair competition and a loss of national sovereignty.

Bolivia is still dependent on loans from international financial institutions such as the International Monetary Fund (IMF) and the World Bank, largely controlled by the United States. The United States has thus put pressure on the Bolivian government to force privatization of strategic resources and eradication of illegal coca cultivation. The American embassy has sometimes intervened in Bolivian politics, enraging some sectors of the Bolivian population. In response to popular demands, new leaders are pursuing a more independent foreign policy stance in relation to the United States.

In January 1992 Bolivia signed an agreement with Peru that granted Bolivia free sea access from the border town of Desaguadero to the Pacific port of Ilo, Peru, until 2091.

ECONOMY

DESPITE ITS MINERAL, oil, and gas wealth, Bolivia is one of the poorest countries in South America and relies on foreign aid, especially from the United States. Bolivia's gross domestic product (GDP) is relatively low at $2,700 per capita income, compared with $13,600 in Argentina and $41,800 in the United States. Many Bolivians live below the poverty line.

There are various reasons why the country remains so poor, including the rugged landscape, which makes transportation and development difficult, and the lack of a direct access to the sea. In addition, the lack of foreign investment has limited the development of Bolivia's economy.

Following two decades of orthodox free-market reform, the economic condition of Bolivian people has worsened. International financial institutions such as the World Bank and International Monetary Fund (IMF) required privatization of the economy. The Bolivian government used the word "capitalization" to sell the concept to the people. As a result of these fiscal adjustments, the Bolivian government lost considerable revenue and was even less able to provide social services.

Opposite: **A night view of the capital city La Paz. La Paz sits in a canyon and is surrounded by snow-capped mountains, with four of the peaks rising higher than 20,000 feet (6,000 m). The city has now outgrown the canyon, spreading out into neighboring valleys and onto the Altiplano.**

INFLATION ALERT

By 1985 inflation in Bolivia was running at 24,000 percent per year. In other words, every item in Bolivia cost 240 times its original price by the end of the year. That means that a candy bar that cost 50 cents on January 1 would cost $120 by December 31!

Under these circumstances nobody wanted to keep their money in the bank, so they either spent it at once or converted it to U.S. dollars. At the height of the inflationary period it cost 1.5 million pesos to buy one U.S. dollar.

Once inflation was under control, the government issued new bank notes in January 1987. The new boliviano replaced the peso as the official currency. One million old pesos were exchanged for one new boliviano.

NATURAL RESOURCES

Bolivia is a poor country in spite of its considerable amount of natural resources. Indeed, the exploitation of such reserves has failed to enrich the economy. Instead of using these natural resources to build internal production capacities, as other countries have, Bolivia has simply sent them out of the country after extraction. This tendency began under the Spanish colonial rule.

Today virtually every valuable mineral is found in Bolivia. Bolivia is a major world producer of bismuth, zinc, and antimony. Gold and silver are also exported. Tin used to be the most important export. The fall in tin prices in the mid-1980s was devastating for Bolivia, where tin is expensive to extract. For every $2.50 the country was paid for tin, it spent $10 to mine and transport it. Many mines were closed and unemployment soared, as 20,000 miners lost their jobs. Mining is now a sector in decline. The Corporación Minera de Bolivia runs the larger mines and leases others to miners' cooperatives.

Another resource is oil. Bolivia's oil fields produce 42,000 barrels a day, but domestic consumption is about 48,000 barrels a day, so oil has to be imported to meet the demand. The oil fields were first developed in the 1920s by the Standard Oil Company of Bolivia, a U.S.–based company. The government took over the fields in 1937. Only after the 1952 revolution did the industry start to receive the investment capital it required.

Recently the natural gas fields were expected to give a boost to the economy. Bolivia uses very little natural gas; most is sold to Argentina and Brazil. Gas pipelines run into Argentina and Brazil. Gas has replaced tin as the top export commodity, and about 3.8 billion cubic yards (2.9 billion cubic m) of gas are exported per year.

Mines, like this tin mine, are common sights all over Bolivia. Tin used to be Bolivia's top export, but has recently been replaced by natural gas. Other minerals in Bolivia are tungsten, antimony, zinc, gold, and silver.

Mining remains a dangerous occupation. In December 1993 a landslide in the Llipi gold fields killed over 200 people.

Gas has become a major economic and political issue. In 2003 an uprising occurred when newly discovered natural gas fields were signed over for export to a multinational consortium. The country's poor, tired of seeing national resources exported without improvement to their own quality of living, erected blockades throughout the country. Gas exploitation was halted in what is now known as the "Gas War."

A "Second Gas War" in 2005, where people demanded nationalization, led to a new political crisis and elections.

The new government has started the state control of natural gas, but must attract the foreign investment needed to develop this important sector.

With its many mountains and rivers Bolivia has considerable potential for producing hydroelectric power. The first projects were built in the vicinity of La Paz and Cochabamba.

Many hillsides are terraced in order to increase arable land. Terraced hillsides in Bolivia go back to the time of the Incas.

AGRICULTURE

Agriculture employs about 40 percent of Bolivians, yet Bolivia cannot grow sufficient food to feed its population. Farming is held back by antiquated methods. On the Altiplano much of the work is still done by hand, and the poor soil barely provides sufficient food for each family to survive. There have been attempts both to modernize agriculture and to bring back some of the successful methods employed by the Incas on the same land.

Bolivia has the second-largest natural gas reserves in South America, after Venezuela.

The more fertile Yungas produce much of the food for La Paz and other cities. These warmer, more fertile areas grow a wider range of fruit and vegetables, including bananas, oranges, turnips, carrots, and cassava, as well as coffee. The Santa Cruz and El Beni departments have over 4 million heads of cattle. The beef is largely for the domestic market, with some exported to Peru and Brazil.

Traditionally the rain forest has added little to the agricultural economy, except for Brazil nuts and latex. There is great potential for extracting tropical hard woods, causing growing conflict between loggers and environmentalists.

INDUSTRY

Because of the small population and the limited spending power of most of the people, Bolivia has only a small market for manufactured goods.

Much of Bolivian industry is still based in small- or medium-sized factories, which produce items to meet daily needs, including textiles, shoes, blankets, and pharmaceuticals. Two-thirds of factories in Bolivia are based in or around La Paz. Santa Cruz and Cochabamba are the other major industrial centers.

Larger factories have been set up to support the mining industry. There are also several oil refineries. Other factories use by-products from oil to produce a wide range of items.

Another important sector is food processing, particularly sugar, coffee, and rice. Bolivian grains such as quinoa are now being promoted in the United States and Europe as health foods. Several cities have large breweries, and local wine is also made in the south of the country.

Bolivia makes many of the products required by the domestic construction industry, and there are brickyards and cement factories. The country has no facilities, however, for heavy industry and has to import motor vehicles and most electrical and consumer goods.

Industry employs about 15 to 20 percent of the workforce, but a great deal of manufacturing takes place in small, family-run workshops employing only two or three people. Such places are seldom registered and operate outside the official figures.

In recent years many new industrial projects have begun operations. These range from a ceramic tile industry in Sucre to a new textile factory in Tarija that combines angora wool with cotton.

WORK ETHIC

Generally, Bolivians are hard workers who take pride in what they do. Many Bolivians are so technically skilled that they can build things from scratch and make complex repairs, but the industrial infrastructure has no place for them and many are forced to seek employment abroad. Unfortunately, people who work with their hands are still looked down on, while doctors, lawyers, and architects, for example, are admired.

People in government employment are often poorly paid, and it is not unusual for them to have second or third jobs, and this sometimes makes it frustrating for people trying to complete paperwork. Government employees often supplement their incomes with bribes.

Bolivian workers can be militant and often try to improve their working conditions through pressure tactics, particularly by striking. Riot police have been called in to break up protests. A consciousness of workers' rights runs through much of Bolivian society, but salaries for the lowest paid workers, such as maids, are not enough to support one person, much less a household.

Some of the hardest workers are indigenous women. In addition to domestic chores, they put in long hours of work on the land or on street corners selling goods to earn extra income for the family.

An estimated 8 percent of the urban population is unemployed, but considerably more are underemployed, doing jobs that do not pay enough to support a family.

Intercity buses are often overcrowded, with people standing, luggage piled up on the roof, and chickens pushed under the seats. In cities buses are supplemented by private minibuses and *trufi* (TROO-fee), cars that drive along set routes, picking up passengers as they go. *Trufi* charge a fraction more than the bus and can be identified by the flags they fly on the hood.

TRANSPORTATION

Bolivia moved from transportation by animals to transportation by airplane without developing the stages in between. Although the road system covers more than 37,755 miles (60,760 km), much of it still needs to be paved. In a country where there is one car per 150 people, cars occupy much of public urban space, making it difficult for pedestrians. Every city has its antiquated bus system and a network of intercity buses that is relatively efficient, given the difficult geography. Hitchhiking is common, and hitchhikers are expected to offer a fare, which is sometimes accepted. Trucks take passengers in the rear open storage area for a "fare," which is cheaper than a bus fare.

Since privatization at the end of the 1990s, Bolivia's passenger train service has been considerably reduced and now covers about 2,187 miles (3,519 km). The western line connects with Chilean railway networks. In the east there is a train connection between Santa Cruz and both Argentina at La Quiaca and Brazil at Corumbá.

In the lowlands Bolivia's navigable rivers offer considerable potential. There is even talk of a major project, the Hidrovía, a river highway that will pass through five countries and link Puerto Suárez in Bolivia to the Rio de la Plate, but the $2 billion project has met with fierce resistance from environmentalists, in part because of the questionable dredging that it would require.

COCA

Coca, sometimes used to make the drug cocaine, is widely believed to be the top Bolivian export. At one point the coca trade was thought to earn Bolivia about $600 million a year. But this figure is only a guess because international trade in coca is illegal and unreported.

Bolivians have been chewing coca and drinking it in tea for centuries. This is legal and an accepted part of the culture. Visiting dignitaries, including the late Pope John Paul II and Queen Sofía of Spain, have tried coca tea. Bolivia makes many coca products, including wine, soap, face cream, medicine, chewing gum, and toothpaste. Whatever the merits of coca itself, when made into cocaine, it becomes dangerous and is illegal.

Most Bolivian coca grows in the Yungas and the Chapare region of North Cochabamba. Coca from the Yungas is used domestically, but the Chapare crop is sometimes shipped to laboratories hidden deep in the rain forest, where it is turned into cocaine. This is sent to Colombia, the center of international cocaine-trafficking rings. From there it is smuggled into the United States and Europe.

Coca eradication programs partly financed by the United States during different governments in the late 1990s led to a near complete stoppage of Chapare coca exports. However, little was done to stop the market for cocaine in the United States and Europe, so coca production merely shifted to Colombia. Coca farmers, many of them former miners who were laid off, were never given viable markets for alternative agricultural products and have thus become even more impoverished. The government elected in December 2005—whose president, Evo Morales, is a former coca grower—has planned for new programs that would industrialize the coca leaf for legal products.

ENVIRONMENT

BOLIVIA'S TROPICAL ANDEAN ENVIRONMENT remains one of the least damaged in the world. The more remote corners of this vast and underpopulated country are hardly touched by human activity. Ironically, because so much has survived, there is so much to protect.

Threats to the environment come in many forms: from the values of different classes of people; from inside the country; or from abroad. Whether the motivation is profit or survival, it is Mother Earth, what many Bolivians refer to as the Pachamama, who pays the price. It is more than wildlife, water, or glaciers that are at stake; it is the lives of people and the existence of whole cultures and ways of life.

Above: **A guide in the Madidi National Park holds a large catfish he caught in the traditional way in the Tuichi River.**

Opposite: **A llama on the Isla de la Luna (Island of the Moon). This island in Lake Titicaca has Incan ruins where young maidens are said to have danced to the moon. It has only about 40 inhabitants and very few boats go there.**

INTERNATIONAL TREATIES

Over the past half century, governments around the world have become more conscious about ecological problems. This environmental conciousness has lead to many treaties meant to protect the environment on an international level. Bolivia has taken part in, signed, and ratified most of these treaties, the most important ones being:

Convention on Biological Diversity; Kyoto Protocol; Convention to Combat Desertification; CITES (Convention on International Trade in Endangered Species of Wild Flora and Fauna); International Tropical Timber Agreement; and Convention on Wetlands of International Importance especially as Waterfowl Habitat.

Elected officials in Bolivia have arrived at a consensus in ratifying most major environmental treaties and have made some inroads in enforcing them at home. However, inaccessible geography, lack of resources, and sometimes simply a lack of political will have weakened enforcement efforts.

A sign to warn people to keep out of the research area for the giant Titicaca frog *(Telmatobius culeus)* at Lake Titicaca.

PROTECTED AREAS

In Bolivia there are dozens of national parks (reserves) spread out around the country. While the definition of a protected area can be debated, at least 15 percent and as much as 35 percent of Bolivia's territory is "protected." Access to such areas is often difficult. Indeed, during the rainy season floods cause communications to be blocked, making it hard to reach many areas within national parks.

The fate of these parks has sometimes led to conflicts. Restricted portions of the protected territory have been granted to local farmers or small entrepreneurs who want to use their resources. However, the government often finds it difficult to enforce antiencroachment laws against people with no such permission to operate in the protected regions. There have also been conflicts with oil companies wanting to exploit parts of the reserves that are the traditional homes of indigenous peoples.

Many national parks are open to visitors. For example there is the park of Torotoro where rock formations and dinosaur prints can be seen. The Cotapata Park near La Paz contains the famous Incan trail, called the Choro, where hikers can trek downward from the Andes to more tropical areas. Visitors can find misty lagoons in the Eduardo Avaroa Park and, in the Sajama Park, the snowcapped Sajama volcano, considered the highest peak of Bolivia. Many parks, including Amboró and Madidi, are the natural habitats of an incredibly wide variety of wildlife.

Bolivia held its first ever National Day of Protected Areas on September 4, 2005. The aim of this annual event is to raise awareness among Bolivians about what a protected area is and how it can benefit the country.

THREATENED SPECIES

Bolivia owes its diversity of plant and animal life to the unparalleled variety of landscapes, from the Andes highlands to the Amazon lowlands. This is home to a great number of endemic animals and plants, meaning species not found anywhere else in the world. At least 79 vertebrates and 4,000 vascular plants exist only in Bolivia, with new species being discovered each year by expeditions of scientists and students.

A condor from the municipal zoo in La Paz. The condor is in danger of becoming extinct because of hunting by Bolivian farmers who claim that the birds kill their sheep and other domestic animals.

While many criticize Bolivia's lack of development and of a road network, which are so essential to economic growth, this is likely what has protected much of the diversity of wildlife that exists in the country. However, this does not prevent many species from being threatened. It can be debated when a species should be considered threatened, and there tends to be a hierarchy of factors for determining which species are the most endangered, leading to categories such as "critically endangered," "endangered," and "vulnerable species."

Bolivia is home to 361 mammal species, 1,414 bird species, 258 reptile species, and 161 amphibian species. Of these, 26 mammal species, 30 bird species, two reptile species, and 21 amphibian species are endangered. Such animals are often threatened by hunters looking for food or for illegal trade. Many specimens of these species, including hyacinth macaws, baby capuchin monkeys, and ocelots, end up as pets, even if it is illegal to keep them in captivity. Bolivian authorities lack resources and determination to apply and enforce laws on protection of wild animals.

Of the identified 17,367 species of vascular plants in the country, 70 are at risk. In addition, 70 of Bolivia's 2,700 species of native trees are threatened. Uncontrolled farming and logging, as well as urbanization, are some of the causes of species endangerment.

Two women survey what is left of their home after a forest fire. According to officials, the fire was caused by slash-and-burn tactics used by farmers. The chaqueo (cha-KAY-oh) is a centuries-old practice of burning portions of tropical forest to prepare fields for agriculture, causing a thick cloud of smoke that fills the Bolivian skies around September of each year. Aside from destroying a part of the forest, this practice also causes air pollution, the effects of which can be seen all the way up in La Paz.

DEFORESTATION

Deforestation is considered a problem in Bolivia precisely because so many forested ecosystems have survived in this biodiverse land, most notably the beautiful cloud forests, which are rare in any part of the world. Around 54 percent of the country—145,149,700 acres (58,740,000 ha)—is covered by forests. In fact, based on statistics from 1994, 78 percent of Bolivia was considered of "low human disturbance," 18 percent of "medium human disturbance," and only 4 percent of "high human disturbance." The deforestation rate was 0.4 percent per year from 1990 to 2000, and 0.5 percent from 2000 to 2005.

Illegal loggers can carry on their business in relative secrecy ironically because of this successful protection of nature, for they can penetrate deep into forests far from any human vigilance. This illegal trade is partly responsible for increasing degrees of deforestation, especially with the exploitation of the endangered hardwood called big-leafed mahogany. No such economy can remain in business without a consumer base, and much of this illegal wood finds its way to U.S. consumers. This one hardwood accounts for more than 50 percent of U.S. imports of tropical wood, and 18 percent of such mahogany imports come from Bolivia.

Given consumer thirst for this product and an impoverished local population in need of the income, government crackdowns on such illegal timber production were largely ineffective. Newer programs attempt to create sustainable models of forest exploitation, such as those sponsored by the World Wildlife Fund and the International Finance Corporation. These and other programs attempt to show loggers that it is in their own best interest to not destroy the very forest that is supporting them. The loss of forests would contribute to other environmental tragedies, such as desertification and the loss of endemic animal and plant species.

The other major factor contributing to deforestation is known as slash-and-burn agriculture, mainly occurring in tropical rain forests. In the 1960s when development was needed, the Bolivian government offered free 75 to 125 acre (30 to 50 ha) plots of land to migrants to clear and farm. But once rain forest land is cleared, the rains wash away the fertility. After two or three harvests the land is no longer worth farming, and these "shifting cultivators" must move to another parcel of land.

Agriculture specialists are attempting to develop a more sustainable agriculture that would permit farming families to remain in the same place and not ravage the surrounding scrublands and forests. Recent experiments with cover crops (those that protect the soil against runoff and provide fertilizing nutrients) attempt to minimize the effects of soil erosion. Farmers in the rain forests and valleys have been using leguminous plants as cover crops. Lowland farmers that were once "shifting cultivators" now have the chance to remain on their fixed plots by rotating rice and bean crops to replenish nitrogen in the soil for the next season of rice.

Some environmentalists challenge whether there is indeed such a thing as "sustainable" logging or agriculture in such rich forests, but until the Bolivian economy creates other job opportunities, pragmatic solutions seem to be the only alternative currently in practice.

About one-fifth of Bolivia's territory is classified as legally conserved, one of the highest rates in the world. It could be argued that the oxygen that these forests provide to the rest of the world is worth some type of compensation. The forests of developed countries, such as those in Europe and North America, have already been largely decimated by development. Thus farmers and loggers in poorer countries consider as hypocritical arguments against their economy coming from developed countries.

Both logging and tourism in their sustainable economic forms are supported by the Bolivian government. In the realm of tourism it is shown that alternatives like "community-based tourism" can give local populations an alternative to woodcutting.

A polluted river in Potosí. The pollution here is caused by industrial waste flowing out from silver mines.

WATER POLLUTION

Water pollution is another form of assault upon the environment. A sad example is the damage done to the Choqueyapu River in La Paz. Situated in a valley, La Paz is full of surface and underground streams, which converge into the Choqueyapu. While in the past it was possible to bathe in its water, rapid urbanization and industrialization have turned it into an open sewer. It is estimated that millions of tons of human litter, and industrial and organic waste are emptied into the river each year.

Though a part of the river-turned-sewer is now covered, much of it is still an ugly sight and smell to people passing by that part of the city. Even in the rich neighborhoods, people have to live with the contamination of the Choqueyapu. As is often the case, the poor people suffer the most from the pollution. Aside from the obvious threat of diseases, many poor people live near the river and use its water to wash clothes or water crops, among other things. Conceivably, residue of the river pollution can find its way onto the fruits and vegetables sold in markets.

One major cause of water pollution is mining, whether from big companies (including one that belonged to former president Gonzálo Sánchez de Lozada) or poor miners desperately trying to make a living.

Often those exploiting mines pay little attention to the environmental consequences. This is what happened with the Pilcomayo River. Water pollution caused by runoff from the mines resulted in poor harvests and high cattle mortality in the region, leading to protests from local farmers.

Investigations revealed that there is indeed a high level of contamination around mines, more than what is legally allowed, and many companies have been put on trial for this.

Small-scale mining is another source of pollution. Ever since the massive layoffs of miners beginning in 1985, some unemployed miners turned to coca growing, while many others joined small and primitively operated mining cooperatives, especially in places where gold might be found. Much of this mining is not regulated by the government, and environmental norms are not respected, which not only leads to negative consequences on miners' health, but also on the environment. This mining activity causes the emission of tons of mercury each year, an extremely toxic element that first affects rivers and eventually reaches the food chain. Possible solutions to this problem include alternative methods for extracting gold, but such methods remain underutilized.

Pesticides, insecticides, and herbicides are other sources of water pollution that can be detrimental to human health. While laws forbidding certain dangerous agrochemicals exist, they are hard to enforce, given the vastness of the country and the limited resources of environmental policing agencies. There are no reliable statistics on pesticide pollution, but the contamination is likely worse than what could be imagined.

However, about 70 percent of Bolivia's agriculture is not intensive or dependent on biotechnology. In this economic sector there is little use of chemical fertilizers, as peasants prefer more traditional methods such as organic fertilizers (compost and manure). While such techniques are hardly competitive on an international level, many environmentalists and advocates of fair trade praise the variety of agricultural production in Bolivia.

Sheep grazing beside a polluted stream in Copacabana.

Substances used in volatile fumigation products, or those containing traces of arsenic, have led to contamination of water sources close to residential areas, such as Lake Titicaca. Some Bolivian scientists fear that underground water sources are also vulnerable.

The consequences of global warming are increasingly evident in Bolivia. The glacier of Mount Chacaltaya lost half of its area and two-thirds of its volume during the last century, and the process is accelerating. This affects the ecosystem since it is the Andean glaciers that largely feed the Amazon rain forest.

BIODIVERSITY

Biodiversity refers to a variety of life in all of its forms, including ecosystems, species, and genetic diversity. Bolivia is part of the tropical Andes, with the most diversity and uniqueness in the world. This has attracted the attention of developed countries interested in the economic and environmental potential of such diverse ecosystems.

Economically, biodiversity provides a country with many resources beneficial to internal and international trade, such as food or pharmaceutical products. The grain quinoa, for example, is becoming trendy in the rest of the world and can be a substitution for other grains, such as rice.

Hidden in Bolivia's remote forests are many plant species yet to be discovered that can prove beneficial to humanity when used as or made into medicine. The country's biodiversity is also good for agriculture since it allows for a variety of crops, acting as a safeguard for farmers. It prevents recessions caused when one-crop economies (monocultures) crumble in the face of plagues or plunging world prices. A diversity of species also works in favor of tourism.

Biodiversity is good for the environment since it enhances soil fertility and prevents erosion, flooding, and other problems. It can also repair some of the damages caused by pollution. This is the case with certain plants that clean up part of the toxicity of the Choqueyapu River once it leaves La Paz. Many scientists strongly believe that a greater genetic diversity gives the ecosystem resilience and eases adaptation to environmental change.

Biodiversity is threatened by human activities such as deforestation and pollution. This may lead to poor agricultural yields. Genetically modified organisms (GMOs) are suspected around the world as posing threats to the agricultural independence of local producers, to the environment, and potentially to public health.

Genetically modified crops such as soy, cotton, and potatoes have already been tested in Bolivia. GMO products are also introduced through imports and foreign aid, especially from the United States. There are regulations on GMOs, but they do not prevent the existence of illegal incursions of altered seeds.

Many Bolivian environmentalists, farmers, and indigenous communities consider GMO products a threat and lobby the government to ban them. Those who defend GMOs argue that it could be beneficial to farmers by improving production, and helpful to the environment since genetically resistant crops are alternatives to pesticides. Some argue that GMOs are a way to fight malnutrition, while others think they are dangerous to health. There is much debate on this. Some fear patents and property rights of big companies over GMOs may strip small farmers of their independence. There is also worry that introducing such industrialized seeds into an environment as rich as Bolivia's could destabilize the ecosystem due to cross pollination between traditional and modified plants.

Farmers in a quinoa field. Nutritionally, quinoa is considered a "super-grain." The World Health Organization has rated the quality of protein in quinoa at least equivalent to that of milk. This crop, native to the Andes, sustained the ancient Incas, and has been cultivated continuously for more than 5,000 years. Quinoa thrives in poor soil, arid climates, and mountainous altitudes.

BOLIVIANS

BOLIVIA HAS A POPULATION of 8,900,000, not a large number for a country so vast. There are fewer people in Bolivia than in Ohio or Florida. However, the population is not evenly distributed. The lowland plains are underpopulated, and 70 percent of all Bolivians live on the Altiplano. Only a little more than half the population resides in cities, a low percentage for a Latin American country.

The Bolivian population is made up of three main groups: Indigenous peoples, mestizos—those with mixed Spanish and indigenous blood—and those who claim to be direct descendants of the Spanish. About 55 percent of the population belongs to the two largest indigenous groups, the Quechua and the Aymará.

The lowland people tend to reflect the warm, sunny weather of their region, with their informal and lively behavior. They usually wear brighter colors and lighter clothes and have the reputation of being the liveliest dancers. Generally thought of as being more adventurous, they also tend to be more business oriented.

Highlanders tend to be conservative and reserved. People from La Paz, for example, are more cautious in their dress and behavior and speak more slowly. Experts from different disciplines have not been able to explain why this highland-lowland dichotomy exists throughout Latin America.

Bolivians are known to be friendly and hardworking. It is interesting to note that Bolivia once had a reputation of providing a safe haven for Nazi war criminals. Although many stories of war crimes are based on rumors, Klaus Barbie, a Nazi Gestapo chief who conducted a reign of terror in southern France, lived in Bolivia for several years. With the participation of the Bolivian government, he was finally extradited to France to face a sentence of life imprisonment. He died in 1991.

Above: **A Quechua girl in La Paz.**

Opposite: **Bolivian girls acting as deputies during a national congress session in La Paz.**

A Quechua man wearing traditional headgear.

THE INDIGENOUS HIGHLANDERS

Bolivia's indigenous highlanders are a rugged, strong-spirited people who have retained much of their culture and identity. The two main groups are the Aymará and the Quechua.

Both groups have slightly larger lungs than average, enabling them to take in more oxygen, and extra blood vessels in their limbs to help keep them warm. The Quechua mainly live in the south of the Altiplano, around Cochabamba, Sucre, and Potosí. The Aymará farm the land around La Paz and Lake Titicaca. The two seldom mix, and intermarriage is rare.

Many from both groups have left the countryside to seek work in cities. Initially the breaking of family ties led to problems from alcohol abuse. People have since adjusted, and the second and third generations, with the advantage of education, have set higher goals in their personal and social struggles to improve their condition.

Although native labor was always important to the economy, indigenous people remain isolated from dominant social sectors. Only since the 1952 revolution have there been attempts to change this, and only in 1975 were Quechua and Aymará made official languages.

THE QUECHUA The Quechua are spread across Peru, Bolivia, and Ecuador. Traditionally they lived in isolated agricultural communities. Recently many have moved to cities to find employment, particularly in construction. The urban Quechua are likely to be bilingual and their lifestyle less traditional.

In more isolated rural communities, the traditional home is a small, one-room building made of sun-dried bricks and a thatched roof. A hearth stands in one corner for the fire. The main highland crop is potatoes, and their livestock usually includes llamas. In valleys the crops are more varied, with corn as a staple. The llamas are rarely slaughtered but are occasionally sold when money is needed. Their wool is woven into shawls and ponchos, which the women weave on traditional peg looms. The family might also keep an alpaca, but its internationally popular wool is more likely to be sold than used for the family.

Looking after the animals is usually the job of the youngest children, who are put to work as soon as they can walk. After the age of 11 or 12, the task of looking after livestock is passed on to younger siblings, and the older children start to help their parents in the fields.

A young Aymará girl. The Aymará are a single group united by one language and a common culture. The Quechua consist of many groups who share the same language but consider themselves culturally distinct. Both the Quechua and Aymará are typically short, with broad faces, dark skin, and black hair.

THE AYMARÁ The Aymará probably arrived at Lake Titicaca sometime between 1400 and 400 B.C. It is likely they came from central Peru, although their arrival in this region is an unsolved historical mystery. They were a fiercely independent people and were able to retain their language after being conquered by the Incas.

The Aymará defend their traditions, and life in rural areas is similar to what it must have been like 1,000 years ago. A typical rural home is built from mud bricks and is either a one-room building or a two-story house. There are likely to be some outbuildings, and the whole complex might be surrounded by a mud-brick wall. A few roofs are still thatched, but corrugated metal is now widely used. Cooking and washing are done outside.

The Aymará grow barley, potatoes, quinoa, beans, onions, and garlic. In the warmer valleys many also produce corn and fruit. Many supplement their diet, or earn a living, from fishing.

THE KALLAWAYA The Kallawaya come from the eastern shore of Lake Titicaca. They are probably related to the Aymará, although their origins are unclear. Legend claims they are direct descendants of the Tiahuanaco who lived there by A.D. 800.

The Kallawaya are farmers and traveling healers. The healers are knowledgeable about the medicinal properties of herbs, using a multitude of plants to effect their cures. The Kallawaya also use spells, charms, and music as holistic aids in their therapies.

The Kallawaya ability to cure is respected throughout Bolivia, and Kallawaya healers can be found all over the country. Several foreign scientists are now studying Kallawaya methods. For the Kallawaya, sickness and disease occur when there is an imbalance of *ajallu* (ah-HAH-yu), or life force.

Because of their nomadic lifestyle, Kallawaya healers tend to be multilingual, able to speak various indigenous dialects as well as Spanish. In addition they have their own "secret" language. A legend claims that because of their healing skills, the Kallawaya were taken to the Incan capital and still speak the language of the ancient royal court.

Kallawaya people are distinguished by the women's woven head-bands and the men's medicine pouches. Their weaving is distinct and colorful. The women wear striped shawls, the colors of which identify the region they are from.

THE CHIPAYA The Chipaya live in one of the most remote parts of the Altiplano, around Coipasa Salt Field. Nobody is sure why they moved to such an inhospitable area, but they probably sought refuge there from the more aggressive Aymará. They now number fewer than 2,000 and mostly live in one village.

The Chipaya look similar to the Aymará but generally have broader faces and darker skin. They tend to wear rough-looking cloth of beige, brown, and black. Chipaya women are easily distinguished by the way they wear their hair in hundreds of small braids.

The Chipaya subsist by farming and herding llamas and sheep. Unlike the Aymará, hunting plays an important part in their lives. Another distinctive feature is the architecture of their simple homes, which are round. The Chipaya surround their villages with mud-built, whitewashed cones, in which offerings are placed to keep evil spirits away.

The Chipaya have accepted some ideas from the outside world, particularly in dress. The men now wear the tight-fitting woolen hats of the Aymará to protect themselves from the cold. They have started to wear simple rubber shoes cut from old car tires.

The Roman Catholic religion has been introduced to the Chipaya but has not replaced traditional beliefs.

A group of Chipaya men sieve for silver in a stream. The Chipaya belong to the Uru people whose origin dates back to 2,000 B.C.

A group of Guaraní people rest in the shade. In 1990, 500 indigenous lowlanders made a dramatic protest march to La Paz. They demanded acknowledgment that 4 million acres (1.6 million ha) of forest belonged to them, new laws to protect them and their forest, and a deadline for logging companies to pack up and leave the Chimanes forest. Under mounting pressure from the protest, the government granted a part of the Chimanes forest to the Guaraní people and drafted an indigenous law to recognize local leaders in that region. Timber companies were required to cease logging activities and were reassigned concessions elsewhere.

THE INDIGENOUS LOWLANDERS

In isolated regions of the lowland plains, particularly in the tropical forests, there are still ethnic groups living traditional lifestyles, isolated from the outside world. These include the Guaraní, Guarayo, and Chiquitano.

Indigenous lowlanders have little in common with the rest of Bolivia. They do not speak the same language, share the same culture, or even look the same. In appearance they tend to be short, dark-skinned people with hair resembling that of peoples of African origin.

Their lifestyles are very simple. They might practice some slash-and-burn farming but generally survive on what the jungle or harsh scrubland provides for them. Technology is limited to a few simple tools and weapons. Houses are usually temporary constructions, and some of the smaller groups do not build homes at all.

Generally the indigenous peoples who lived along the rivers enjoyed the most favorable environment and developed the more advanced cultures, including complex and impressive canal systems for irrigating

THE SIRIONÓ

The Sirionó, who are part of the Guaraní group of people, live in the tropical forests of Bolivia. Like most of the forest peoples, they are short; even the men seldom grow taller than 5 feet 4 inches.

Even as recently as 30 years ago the Sirionó lived a traditional existence. The men were skillful hunters, catching armadillos, monkeys, and tortoises. They also caught fish with a bow and arrow.

Both men and women gathered fruit and other food from the surrounding rain forest, but other work was strictly segregated between men and women. Hunting, house building, and tree chopping were men's work. Weaving, caring for the children, cooking, and twining hammocks were considered women's work. Decision making is mostly done collectively.

At that time, the Sirionó apparently had no knowledge of making fire. Anthropologists who stayed in a Sirionó village watched them carefully protect glowing embers whenever the village moved its site, but they were never seen to start a new fire.

Sirionó art mainly consisted of elaborate body painting. They also had their own music and dances, and with the sunrise the whole village would wake and start singing. Dancing was an evening activity. However, the Sirionó would never dance on moonless nights.

Today there are about 1,500 Sirionó surviving in several different areas. In 1992 the government put aside a reserve for them, but in many ways their isolation has been broken. Agriculture plays an increasing role in their lives, and it is not uncommon to see them wearing western clothing.

In towns people often use the word chola *(CHOH-lah) to refer to indigenous women who wear traditional dress. It is acceptable to say to a third person, "Look at those* cholas *over there," but rude to call an individual a* chola *to her face.* Cholita *(choh-LEE-tah) carries more affection and is sometimes used to address a person one is familiar with.*

crops and for transportation. It was also these people who had the first contact with the Europeans, and therefore their culture has undergone the most drastic change. Many indigenous groups have abandoned their old ways of life and found work in the river settlements or rubber plantations.

The Bolivian government once offered free land to families willing to move from the crowded Altiplano to the lowlands. Thus now even the most remote peoples, who had previously managed to retain their isolated lifestyles, are finding themselves threatened as new roads are cut through the forest.

THE SPANISH

A significant number of people in Bolivia still claim to be directly descended from the early Spanish colonists. Some, with vestiges of colonialist mentality, refer to themselves as *blancos* (BLAN-kohs), meaning whites. Among these, the ones from the most conservative of prominent families refer to themselves as *la gente decente* (la HAIN-tay day-SAIN-tay), meaning "the decent people," or *la gente buena* (la HAIN-tay BWAY-nah), meaning "the good people."

It is hard to estimate how many people fall into this exact category because there has been much intermingling of the races. After four centuries, many of those who claim to be 100 percent Spanish could probably find indigenous or other blood somewhere in their family history. In the past this group was remarkably homogeneous and fiercely protective of their Spanish heritage. As a result there is a distinct group who are light-skinned and indistinguishable in appearance from people who have never left Spain.

The old-fashioned concept of "being Spanish" is made up of a combination of factors, of which purity of blood is just one. Other characteristics of being Spanish include a sense of aristocracy, a code of moral behavior, a high level of education, fluency in Spanish, European attitudes toward work, and pride in the Spanish heritage.

Although numerically small, the people of this group still have considerable influence in economics and politics. Their lifestyle generally includes all the modern luxuries. With servants and large mansions or apartments, many enjoy a higher standard of living than most North Americans. However, many Bolivians of Spanish descent have come to terms with the fact that they live in a country of cultural diversity, and give credit to Bolivia's indigenous heritage.

A little boy with distinctive Spanish coloring is dressed for his baptism.

THE MESTIZOS

The mestizos are people of mixed Spanish and indigenous blood. They make up about one-third of the Bolivian population. They are traditionally far more likely to speak and write Spanish than the pure-blooded indigenous population and therefore have found it easier to become part of mainstream Bolivian society.

Many people of mixed blood still make their living from selling handicrafts, trading, and running small businesses. Since 1952 many mestizos have taken advantage of better educational opportunities, and now people of mixed blood are well established in all the major professions. Indeed they have the reputation of being shrewd at business, and there are countless legends of the wealth of the mestizos. Other Bolivians believe that even the scruffy-looking mechanic who fixes their car probably has numerous deals in the fire and a fortune in the bank.

In modern Bolivian society a few successful mestizos have even broken through Bolivia's strong class divide and become accepted into *blanco* society. At the same time mestizo people often retain a respect for their traditions and background. The mestizo and indigenous labels probably reflect cultural customs more than racial composition.

Young city dwellers. Social position is determined by many other factors in addition to race, including the ability to speak Spanish, whether they live in an urban area and work in a white-collar job, and their social behavior.

An Afro-Bolivian from the Yungas.

THE AFRO-BOLIVIANS

In the 16th century the Spanish brought slaves from Africa to work in the mines. The Africans were unable to adjust to the cold Altiplano climate and were resettled in the Yungas, where they worked as farmers. Up until the 1952 revolution their descendants were still working under near-slavery conditions. People alive today can remember being made to work in the fields when they were only 6 or 7 years old and being whipped if they did not work hard enough.

Today there are an estimated 17,000 descendants of former slaves living in Bolivia, but such estimates greatly vary from one researcher to another. They speak Spanish with a sprinkling of African words, and those around La Paz are quite likely to speak Aymará as well. Some of the women have even adopted the Aymará habit of wearing bowler hats.

Bolivians of African origin are still subject to subtle racism, with few of them attending college or holding influential positions. They have been able to make more of an impact in sports and music, and one of the few legacies of their African background is *saya* (SIE-ah) music. Consisting of chants, dancing, and rhythmic drum beats, this African sound has been passed down from generation to generation. It has even crossed over into Bolivian mainstream culture. *Saya* rhythms and chants are used by fans at soccer matches.

In 1982 high school students in the Yungas created the Afro-Bolivian Cultural Movement to preserve their culture, and today special Afro-Bolivian concerts are often featured on national television.

NEW ARRIVALS

Over the years Bolivia, with its great untapped potential, has attracted various waves of immigrants seeking a better life. The arrival of new groups has often resulted from upheavals in another part of the world. The persecution of Jews before and during World War II led to a number of Polish and German immigrants going to Bolivia. They tended to center in La Paz and Cochabamba, although many later moved on to Peru, Argentina, or Israel.

Postwar poverty in Japan resulted in a group of Okinawan farmers emigrating to the department of Santa Cruz. The new arrivals had to carve their homesteads out of the rain forest. At first life was very hard. The nearest town was two days away by horse, floods destroyed their first crops, and people died from the unhealthy forest climate.

Second- and third-generation Japanese-Bolivians tend to think of themselves as Bolivians, but with strong Japanese ties.

Since then the community has prospered, and today their small towns are home to nearly 2,000 people of Japanese background and about twice as many Bolivians. The community has hospitals built with Japanese government aid, and the city of Santa Cruz is now just a few hours away on a good road.

Japanese immigrants introduced some new agricultural ideas to Bolivia, particularly rice growing and poultry farming. Today this small area produces half of Bolivia's poultry and eggs and enough rice to have a surplus for export.

The Okinawans still maintain their Japanese culture and language, and many of the children are sent to Japan for their university education.

LIFESTYLE

LIFE IN THE RURAL AREAS of Bolivia has not changed much since Incan times. This is particularly true on the Altiplano, the heartland of the country. Making a living in this harsh environment requires using all the resources available. The economy still centers around livestock.

There is not much plant variety on the Altiplano, and virtually everything that grows is put to use. *Thola* and *yareta* are used for fuel, *ichu* is the main food for the llamas, and eucalyptus trees provide fuel and wood for building houses and making furniture.

One of the most useful plants is the *totora* reed, which grows around Lake Titicaca. These reeds can be dried for fuel, fed to the livestock, or made into small boats. The boats are mainly used for fishing, and they last less than a year before the reeds start to rot and the boat has to be replaced. Many people now have boats made from wood or fiberglass, and reed boatbuilding is becoming a dying art.

Llamas might look like harmless and cuddly animals, but they have nasty tempers and sometimes bite and spit at people who get too close.

Left: **Llamas are particularly important to highland farmers. They provide meat, wool, and leather; they are used for transport; and their dried dung makes excellent fuel. Most Altiplano families keep a herd of llamas.**

Opposite: **Harvesting quinoa. Farming, which employs nearly half the population, is hampered by the poor soils of the Altiplano.**

Beggars in La Paz. A rural drought in the 1980s brought waves of beggars into La Paz. Even after the drought, some stayed on in the city and many now return each year. They can usually make enough money begging to purchase some basic items such as pots and pans before returning to their villages.

URBAN POOR

The 1952 revolution gave farmers the land they worked, but usually they have no ownership papers for the property. As such, their land cannot be sold. This means that farmers have to divide their land among their sons, so for each generation the plots of land get smaller and the people poorer. As a result, many indigenous farmers leave to seek work in the cities. The new arrivals stay with relations in the poorer neighborhoods, where living conditions are often basic, with little sanitation or heating.

Many people in low-income groups work in factories or mines. The women become street vendors, selling fruit, vegetables, or weavings, or even factory-made items ranging from plastic toys to computer disks.

Life for children of the poorest Bolivians in urban communities is worse than in rural areas, and young children often spend their days sitting on the street corner while their mothers work. Some homeless and orphaned children sleep on the street and work as shoeshine boys or as *voceadores* (voh-say-ah-DOR-ays). *Voceadores* work on the buses, shouting out stops and collecting fares. Increasingly, shelters are available for these children, sponsored by nongovernmental organizations.

COCA—PART OF LIFE

To most indigenous highlanders, the coca leaf is more than a luxury; it is an essential commodity of life, and survival would be hard without it. The leaves are a mild narcotic and chewing them helps to numb cold, pain, and hunger. Coca is also used as a medicine.

According to legend, the indigenous people once tried to burn a clearing to build their homes, but the fire got out of hand and burned down part of the forest. This made the gods angry, and they sent down a thunderstorm to put out the fire. By the time the storm was over, only one tough little plant, the coca, had survived. The people chewed its leaves and found it gave them nourishment and helped them forget the hardship they had brought upon themselves.

THE MINERS

Bolivia mines gold, silver, tin, and other minerals. Some mines are owned by the miners themselves and operated as cooperatives. Life is often hardest in these mines because there is little money to invest in equipment. Most of the work is done using hand tools, with miners working in narrow, unventilated, and unbearably hot passageways.

Although no one under the age of 18 is supposed to work in the mines, boys as young as 12 or 13 are sometimes taken on as helpers. After three or four years, they can apply to the cooperative to become miners.

Generally the miners gather early in the morning at the mine and linger outside, drinking tea and chewing coca to prepare themselves for the day ahead. Once underground they may work for nine hours before returning to the surface. Miners in cooperative mines set their own dynamite to loosen the rock. It can take two or three hours just to chisel out a hole for the dynamite. After the explosion the tunnel is full of dangerous fumes, and while waiting for these to disperse, the miners take a coca break. Miners believe that chewing coca not only gives them energy but also filters out some of the harmful fumes they breathe in.

Miners in government mines are better off, and they have a reputation of being very militant, often striking over bad conditions, and sometimes getting involved in politics.

All miners, whether in cooperative or state-owned mines, have a hard and dangerous job. Even if they are lucky enough to avoid accidents, working in the mines almost inevitably leads to serious lung disease, and many miners die before they reach 50.

TRADITIONAL DRESS

The traditional indigenous dress of homemade trousers and poncho is now seldom worn by men on the Altiplano; they are far more likely to wear factory-made trousers, jackets, and shirts. Traditional hats are even being replaced by baseball caps, although this fashion is popular so far only among boys and young men. For many people, *chullas* (CHOO-lahs)—woolen caps with ear flaps—remain popular, if only because they are so practical in the cold weather. The handknit *chullas* are exported to Europe.

Traditional dress is still widely worn by indigenous women. Aymará women are reasonably uniform in their attire, but the Quechua show more variation, particularly in hats. They wear an apron over a long skirt with many underskirts. This makes the outer skirt stick out like a hoopskirt and keeps the women warm. They are worn with an embroidered blouse, a cardigan, and a shawl called a manta (MAHN-tah). A vital part of the outfit is the *quepi* (k-epi). These colorful rectangles can be folded to make a pouch at the back to carry shopping or babies. Home-woven cloth is now giving way to brightly colored factory-made material.

Women generally wear their hair in one long braid down the back. The final touch is a hat, which is very important on the Altiplano because it gives protection from the strong winds and unfiltered sun. Across Bolivia there is a wide range of headwear, but the favorite for Aymará women is the bowler hat, known locally as the *bombin* (bohm-BEEN). The bowler hat may have been introduced to Bolivia by British railway workers, although why Aymará women rather than men started wearing them is a mystery.

Another story, probably only a legend, tells that a shipment of bowlers was sent to Bolivia by mistake and the owner sold them to the Aymará women by promising the hats would bring them fertility. For many years the Borsalino factory in Italy made hats almost entirely for the Bolivian market, although today they are produced locally.

Certain public figures proudly wear the typical *pollera* (po-YER-ah) skirt and its accessories. However, many young women are shedding the traditional dress in exchange for contemporary styles as part of western Bolivian social developments.

ALTITUDE SICKNESS

In the high altitude of the Altiplano (12,000 feet or 3,660 m), oxygen density is lower than most visitors are used to. The first thing noticed is that a newcomer starts breathing heavily after even light exercise, such as walking upstairs. This delivers more oxygen but also puts more carbon dioxide in the blood. The victim may experience loss of appetite, feel tired, get headaches, or find thinking to be muddled.

This altitude sickness is known locally as *sorojchi* (so-ROH-shay). After a couple of days these symptoms fade. People not born at high altitude will never fully adjust, as sports teams coming to play in La Paz quickly discover. Even the local people respect the altitude they live at and walk slowly. Bolivians who are not used to daily hard work also breathe heavily if they suddenly have to exert themselves.

HEALTH CARE

Health is a major issue in Bolivia. The nation has only a small budget for health care. Good medical schools produce doctors that many Bolivians cannot afford. A two-tiered system provides modern health care for the wealthy and middle class, while an underfunded public health system makes do with doctors earning working-class salaries. With little investment in rural areas, urban medical care is far superior to rural clinics. Rural Bolivians often turn to folk remedies. On the average Bolivian men live to be 63, and women 68. In the United States the averages are 75 years for men and 81 for women. Infant mortality is also high, with 53 out of every 1,000 Bolivian babies dying. This compares with seven out of 1,000 in the United States and 15 out of 1,000 in neighboring Argentina.

The government has put most of its limited resources into combating malaria and dysentery, though other diseases are receiving increasing attention. One of these is Chagas's disease, thought to have infected more than a million Bolivians. This disease is caused by a bug that lives in cracked walls and roofs of poorly constructed homes. At night it bites people while they sleep and sucks their blood. The feces of the insect contains a parasite that can enter the victim's body if the bite is scratched. The parasite then works itself slowly into the bloodstream. There might be some immediate signs, such as fever or swelling, but these pass. The parasite, however, remains in the blood, and years later it attacks the heart and digestive system, resulting in what appears to be sudden death.

Poor hygiene and a lack of sanitation in rural areas result in frequent dysentery and worm infections. In the lowlands malaria is a constant danger.

Above: **In the past the government felt that Bolivia was underpopulated and tended to stay clear of the subject of birth control. The Roman Catholic Church also opposes most forms of birth control.**

Opposite: **A child being baptized. Godparents are selected for baptism, and these become lifelong ties in which the godparents take responsibility for the younger person's physical and spiritual well-being.**

BIRTH AND FAMILY PLANNING

In the past family planning was largely ignored in Bolivia. Some private agencies worked with the rural population, but the government did not get involved. The latest government has been more willing to consider the issue, and it acknowledges that family planning is important.

Traditionally, low-income Bolivian women breastfeed their children for a long period, sometimes up to two years. While they are breastfeeding, women are less likely to become pregnant again, and this has traditionally helped to space out additions to the family. However, the increasing use of bottle-feeding disrupts this natural pattern.

Many poor women give birth at home, often without proper consideration for hygiene. Midwives, called *matronas* (mah-TROH-nahs), attend to the mother. Although they are experienced, they have no medical training. Urban women from higher income groups can either have their baby in a hospital or have a doctor in attendance at home. The hospital is the usual choice.

Although birth control and sex education are more available in urban areas, rural Bolivians have less access to contemporary family planning. Ever since the Peace Corps was expelled from Bolivia in the early 1970s following suspicions that they were covertly sterilizing highland women, family planning has been a sensitive issue in rural areas.

PADRINOS

Padrinos (pah-DREE-nohs), or godparents, play a central role for many Bolivians. To be selected as a godparent is a great honor. Rich families use the padrino system to build ties with people of equal status. Poor people might ask someone of higher status, perhaps a boss at work, to be their child's *padrino*. A *padrino* who owns a factory could not refuse to give his godchild a job, nor could he see him or her miss school because of poverty. In rural areas it is traditional for landowners, merchants, or politicians to accept many *padrino* commitments. This cements their position in society.

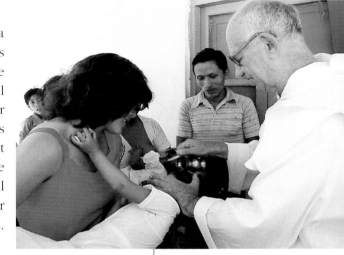

CHILDHOOD AND GROWING UP

The first years of childhood for many Bolivian children from low-income families are spent either strapped onto their mother's back or crawling around the ground playing while she works.

A hair-cutting ceremony takes place at around 2 years of age, which is when many children are weaned. The child's hair is braided into lots of tiny pigtails, each tied with a ribbon. The first of these locks is cut by the *padrinos*. Other relations then take turns to cut a small piece of hair according to their age and rank in the family. Each person presents the child with a gift of money, which is pinned onto the child's clothes. In rural society this money is used to buy animals. People say that crops may die, but livestock is capital for life. Herds of llamas or sheep are often tagged on the ear in different colors to mark which of the children in the family they belong to.

At 18 boys are supposed to do a year's service in the army. Middle-class and wealthy boys often do alternative services, while some with great influence receive their military ID without serving at all. Poorer Bolivians use the military for learning skills. When they return, they are considered to have become men, and their safe return is celebrated with a large party.

Cutting the cake. For children there are often two parties, the first at school, either just before or just after class, the second at home.

BIRTHDAYS

Birthdays are big family occasions in Bolivia, and most people, whatever their age, will hold a party. Often adults have the party on the exact day rather than wait for the weekend, even though parties tend to go on until late at night. For adult parties, guests are free to arrive at any time in the evening, but they should arrive an hour or more after the time of the invitation.

It is not socially acceptable to arrive at the exact time of the invitation because the host has already incorporated the usual lateness of guests in the mentioned hour. Generally everybody brings their children along. There is dancing, probably a meal around 11:00 P.M., and the cutting of the cake at midnight.

It is common to celebrate a child's birthday on the weekend, usually on a Saturday, starting around noon. There are light refreshments, probably *salteñas* (sal-TAY-nyahs), small, spicy meat and vegetable pies, and perhaps hot dogs, because some children do not like the spicy *salteñas*.

Most people bring a small gift to the party—a toy for children or chocolates or a bottle of wine for adults. The wrapped gifts are put aside to be opened later. As Bolivian people do not ordinarily put their names on these gifts, the person celebrating a birthday might not remember who gave what present. It is beginning to become customary to open the gift in front of the giver as it is received.

WEDDINGS

In the countryside it is common for people to live together, usually in the man's family house, before marrying. Generally after a festival, a man will persuade a woman to move in with him. This is called "stealing the girl." In the days that follow, the two families meet and negotiate the union, and then exchange gifts. The couple might stay together for years and have children before they have saved enough for a wedding with a priest and a celebration with their family and neighbors.

In urban areas Aymará, Quechua, and mestizo weddings are great occasions. Saturday is the traditional day to get married. After the service the couple stands on the church steps and the guests take turns offering congratulations. The bride and groom then climb into a taxi that has been specially rented and decorated for the occasion. The best man jumps into the front seat and the parents into the back until there are six or seven people inside, not including the driver. The other guests climb into a waiting bus, and the wedding party reassembles at a local hall for a celebration.

A wedding procession. It is traditional in rural society for the couple to lead a procession from the church to the bride's home for a banquet.

75

Schoolchildren in Bolivia. The middle classes place considerable emphasis on education, whereas in rural communities the dropout rate is high.

EDUCATION

Education in Bolivia is free, universal, and technically compulsory. However, children in rural communities are also expected to do their share of the work on the farm, so many children drop out of school before finishing their elementary education. Urban child laborers also often miss school for economic reasons, and enforcement of compulsory education becomes difficult in such cases.

There are also cultural reasons for school dropouts. Classes are conducted in Spanish, which many indigenous children find difficult to understand. However, much progress has been made. In the 1990s bilingual education was incorporated in an increasing number of rural schools. According to official statistics, Bolivia has reached 95 percent of primary school attendance, but these statistics do not take the dropout rate into consideration.

Middle school lasts three years and high school, which is not compulsory, lasts 4 years. Most secondary schools are located in towns and cities, so it is very difficult for rural children to attend. Some families arrange for sons to go and live in a town with another family. That host family virtually owns the boy, who must work for them when he comes back from school. It is a very hard system but does allow a few boys from rural backgrounds to graduate. Most rural families will not permit their daughters to live away from home, which denies them the chance of a secondary education.

There has been much progress with literacy over the years, as now about 87 percent of the population can read, though this varies widely between different social classes as well as between men and women. The literacy rate is 93 percent for men and 82 percent for women.

The primary obstacle in Bolivian education concerns the huge gap in quality of education and class size between well-financed private schools and an overextended public system, in which grossly underpaid teachers cope with large class sizes and poor facilities. Until this two-tiered system is reformed, the lack of equal access to education will inhibit Bolivia's economic and social progress.

FUNERALS

Funerals are emotional affairs with usually a great deal of sobbing and visible grief. The preferred time for a funeral to be held is 3:00 P.M. After the service close friends carry the coffin out of the church and then walk two or three blocks, with the other guests following. After a set distance the coffin is put in a hearse for the rest of the journey to the cemetery.

Poor families will find the money to pay for a funeral for an adult, even if they have to borrow it. However, as child mortality is high, a child's funeral might take a different format. A member of the family is sent to buy a casket while the family washes and dresses the child's body and lays it on a table. They use their own candles and flowers to decorate the room.

It is usual to let other children climb onto the table to touch and kiss the body because this is their way of saying goodbye and understanding what has happened.

A cemetery in La Paz. The Chipaya consider themselves the oldest race in the world and are known as "the people of the tombs." This is because of the stone towers, or chullpas (CHOOL-pahs), that were once used to house the skeletons of their ancestors.

ROLE OF WOMEN

The rights of women are well protected by Bolivian law, but cultural and social traditions continue to hold women back.

Women do not always benefit from the laws that are there to protect them. For example, Bolivian women are entitled to three months' maternity leave. However, many women in low-paying jobs are unaware of this or afraid of losing their jobs if they take the time off.

From childhood, indigenous girls are brought up to be submissive and conservative, and although women make major contributions to the economy, they generally remain subordinate to their fathers

For working-class women in Bolivia, life is likely to consist of continuous hard work, giving birth to children, and caring for the family.

and husbands. As a result they rarely get the chance to participate in the village meetings where decisions are made or to benefit from training programs. If they are widowed, it can be difficult for them to run the farm on their own because officials are sometimes reluctant to give them the important agricultural loans for seeds and equipment.

Unemployment is another factor that blocks female emancipation. Since it is difficult for them to find a job, women have to live with their parents until they get married as they depend on their financial support.

La Paz schoolgirls. Even in established urban families, where all children are likely to be sent to school, it is common for parents to send their sons to better private schools and their daughters to government schools.

Women are often subjected to domestic violence. In the countryside much of this goes unreported, but in the cities it has become a far greater issue and has generated much social awareness.

In middle-class society women have previously remained largely economically inactive. This is changing rapidly, and more and more Bolivian women are moving into high-profile leadership roles.

RELIGION

WHEN THE SPANISH ARRIVED in Bolivia, they brought the Roman Catholic religion with them, and today 95 percent of the population is classified as Catholic. However, Catholicism is mixed with indigenous beliefs, which still have a strong hold in the indigenous communities. Bolivian people say that they have one foot in the church and one foot in tradition.

In the last 40 years the Roman Catholic Church has ventured into the fields of social work and education. During some of the more oppressive dictatorships, certain Church officials, often under the influence of liberation theology (a religious doctrine favoring grassroots social reform), have spoken up powerfully for human rights. In 1980 Archbishop Jorge Manrique of La Paz opened an office to help political prisoners, while the Catholic newspaper Presencia and the Jesuit Radio Fides were attacked by government paramilitaries and temporarily shut down because of the outspoken journalism of some reporters.

About 5 percent of the population is considered Protestant, which includes Methodists, Episcopalians, Baptists, Jehovah's Witnesses, and Mormons. The Protestant faiths are gaining some ground in indigenous communities and in the cities.

The old Catholic churches are important landmarks, and the squares in front of them form meeting places and trading centers. In the cities Bolivian churches are generally active and lively places, with people continually coming and going.

Above: **A Roman Catholic church in Toledo.**

Opposite: **The Moorish interior design of a cathedral in Copacabana. People come to pray before a favorite statue, light candles, or just sit and meditate.**

Incas worshipping the sun. As they conquered other cultures, the Incas did not necessarily suppress their religions, but they demanded that Inti rule over the local gods.

THE INCAN RELIGION

Before the Spanish arrived, the Incas had their own religion. They believed in many different gods, built temples to honor them, and trained priests to oversee the worship. There is a great deal we do not know about the Incan religion, but it seems to have been a combination of nature worship, theological notions, animistic beliefs, and magic.

The supreme god in the Incan religion was Inti, the sun god. The emperor was seen as the son of Inti, so that worship of Inti was tied in with worshipping the emperor. Inti's wife was Mamaquilla, the moon goddess. Pachamama ruled over the earth, Mama Cocha was the mother of the sea, and Illapa was the god of thunder and rain.

The earth was created by Viracocha, who first made giants, then, when he was unhappy with them, turned them into stone. He then came out of Lake Titicaca to create a new race, humans. Gradually, Viracocha appears to have become more important than Inti. Various historians have tried to guess the reasons for this development, but no one really knows.

The agricultural seasons were particularly important to the Incas, and great religious festivals were held at all the important stages of the farming season. People were expected to provide food and labor for the gods, and sacrifices of animals were made. Human sacrifices also took place, particularly at times of major uncertainty and upheaval, but this offering was a rare event and conducted only in the main temples.

THE OLD GODS SURVIVE

The old gods, who date back to pre-Spanish (also called pre-Columbian) times, are still part of the culture of many Bolivians. Whether people believe in them as gods, as superstition, or simply as part of their folklore that they wish to keep alive is debatable.

There is certainly a serious respect for Pachamama, the Incan earth mother, which Quechua society associates with the Virgin Mary. Pachamama protects people, animals, and plants but can also be cruel and revengeful. Pachamama presides over all major events, such as marriages or giving birth, but she must also be considered when it comes to more mundane actions, such as chewing the first coca of the day.

El Tío (TEE-oh) is the ruler of hell and owner of minerals. Miners place small ceramic figures of El Tío in niches in the passageways into their mine. This figure is offered coca, cigarettes, and alcohol to keep him happy. He is never referred to as the devil, but always as Tío, which means "uncle."

Pachamama has the first right to all things, and whenever people start drinking alcohol, a little liquid is poured on the ground for her. Indigenous people carefully place a little chewed coca on the road as an offering before undertaking a journey. She is also honored when the first furrows are dug and at the completion of a new building.

Ekeko, which means "dwarf" in Aymará, is a pleasant little household god who retains a role in Bolivian daily life. Figurines of Ekeko portray him as a round-faced, grinning little figure laden with kitchen items. He is responsible for finding wives and husbands, for endowing good luck in business, and for providing homes. He is particularly revered in mestizo culture.

The Jesuit church in Santa Cruz. The Jesuits gave the indigenous people the opportunity of having an education and also taught many practical skills. The region became famous for its wood carvings and other works of art.

INFLUENCE OF THE JESUITS

For many years the government in the high plateau had little interest in the lowlands. Instead this area was developed by Jesuit priests, who came across the border from Paraguay. They set up around 30 communities throughout the region, each with a few priests to run them and a contingent of soldiers for protection.

The Jesuits were quite zealous in imposing their type of Catholicism on the indigenous population, and in doing so they destroyed much of the culture that had once existed in this region. In its place they introduced Spanish culture, and this still shows in the local music, which is quite different from anywhere else in Bolivia. However, when local people under Jesuit tutelage created works of art, indigenous motifs were superimposed into the Spanish baroque style.

The Jesuit communities were well run and prosperous. The priests grew cotton, sugarcane, corn, yucca, rice, and many other fruits and vegetables. They also brought in cattle and horses. Trade grew between the lowlands and the highlands. Sugarcane, other crops, and finished works of art were exchanged for silver. The missions and their armed soldiers also protected the local people from Brazilian slave traders.

For many years the area was virtually an autonomous religious state, forming a buffer zone between the Spanish and Portuguese in South America. Eventually the Jesuits become too powerful, and the Spanish kings started to become suspicious of their activities and jealous of their wealth. Thus, in 1767 all Jesuit priests were expelled from the continent.

MIRACLES AND PILGRIMAGES

Legend has it that in the small village of Quillacollo in 1770, the youngest daughter of a poor family had the task of looking after the sheep. One day, while out in the fields, she met a beautiful woman carrying a little baby. The young girl and the woman met many times, and the daughter so enjoyed their talks that she often returned home late.

Her family did not believe her story, so one day they followed her. Seeing her parents the daughter cried out *"Ork' hopiña,"* which in the Quechua language means "She is already on the mountain." With this cry the woman and baby disappeared before the eyes of the startled parents. The news spread around the village, and the people who rushed to the spot found a small image of the Virgin Mary. Today that image can be found in the village church, and every year on August 15, it is paraded around the village.

There is an important pilgrimage to Copacabana each year. The town is overlooked by a tall, steep hill called the Cerro Calvario, which has been marked out with the stations of the cross. At dusk on Good Friday, there is a candlelight procession from the cathedral to the top of the hill.

Pilgrims to the Cerro Calvario place stones on each cross, and at the top of the hill they pray and burn incense. They also leave miniature models of items they hope to acquire in the months ahead. Some people even walk the 90 miles (150 km) from La Paz as part of this pilgrimage.

CHA'LLA

A *cha'lla* (CHAH-ya) is a ritual blessing. It might be a Catholic event, a ceremony drawn from indigenous religion, or as is often the case, a combination of the two. It is conducted by a *yatiri* (yah-TEE-ree), spiritual leader, or a Catholic priest.

A *cha'lla* ceremony is performed whenever a new building is started or completed, for otherwise there will never be peace in that building. The ceremony takes place on a Saturday. The owner of the building and the workers prepare an offering, called a *cucho* (KOO-choh), consisting of a wax man, grains of incense, aromatic herbs, a few leaves of coca, cotton still on the branch, tin figures of humans and animals, and household objects, all sprinkled with an alcoholic drink.

One of the workers presides over the ceremony if a *yatiri* or a priest is not available. He is left alone with the *cucho*, which he burns. He watches the way the smoke rises to be sure all the evil spirits have left. He also asks Pachamama for her blessing. When the others return, the ashes from the offerings and any chewed coca are placed in a sack and buried in the foundations. From then on the *cucho* is the invisible guardian of the building.

WITCHCRAFT AND WISDOM

The *yatiri* is the local shaman who can be hired to help with problems. They often conduct services very much like priests. If you were visiting a holy place, you might ask a *yatiri* to conduct a small service first. The *yatiri* will burn incense, sing chants, and make an offering to Pachamama to make sure your visit goes smoothly. If seeking advice on matters such as marriage or a business venture, clients might ask a *yatiri* to tell their fortune. A fortune is often predicted by reading coca leaves. The fortune teller talks to the spirits, and then spreads a handful of leaves on a cloth to derive clues about the future from the shape they form. Fortune telling conducted this way might also be used to locate lost items or people.

Amauta (ah-MOW-tah) are wise men. In Incan society the *amauta* had to remember vast amounts of information because there were no written records. They are still respected for their wisdom.

Many people believe in harmful spirits. *Karisirus* are night phantoms who catch people out after dark or when they are sleeping. According to legend, they split their victim's stomach and extract some of the fat.

La Paz has a whole street known as the witches' market, where they sell herbs, seeds, and various animal parts, including dried llama fetuses, which should be placed under the cornerstone of any new building.

In rural areas mothers calling their children indoors shout a warning about the karisirus *to make them come home quicker.*

LANGUAGE

BOLIVIA HAS THREE OFFICIAL LANGUAGES: Spanish, Aymará, and Quechua. In addition there are dozens of isolated languages that are each spoken by a few thousand people. Various waves of immigrants have also added to this mixture. In a few lowland towns, one could probably communicate just as easily in Japanese as in Spanish.

Although the Aymará and Quechua languages have acquired a new status, Spanish remains the most important language of commerce, art, broadcasting, and politics. About two-thirds of the population speaks Spanish as their first language. Although Aymará and Quechua are very widespread, most indigenous people speak Spanish too.

Opposite: **Magazines and newspapers on display at a newspaper stand. Spanish is the language used for most newspapers.**

Below: **Public typists set up shop on the sidewalk.**

89

QUECHUA AND AYMARÁ

Bolivia's other two official languages are Quechua and Aymará. As these languages are quite similar in technical points, such as the way words are compounded, linguists believe they might be related. Indeed someone who does not speak either language might listen to them and think they were the same. The vocabulary, however, is very different, and Quechua and Aymará speakers cannot understand each other.

In the past, few Spanish speakers bothered to learn either of these Andean languages, preferring that the indigenous population learn Spanish. With interest increasing in indigenous culture, this situation is slowly changing. However, even Spanish speakers who are willing to try to learn one of their nation's other official languages do not necessarily find it easy to do so. The sound of both Aymará and Quechua is very different from most European languages, and this makes them difficult for Spanish speakers to learn. There are also other differences. For example, the power and force with which some sounds are delivered are an important part of the communication, as is leaving a slight pause between some sounds.

The major Bolivian media do little to cater to Aymará and Quechua speakers, although radio and television do give the news in the two indigenous languages. These programs are usually broadcast early in the morning, before the farming community starts work. One radio program even carries personal messages, uniting family members who live far apart. Enterprising Aymarás and Quechuas have created local community radio stations that serve their immediate regions.

Two indigenous men conversing.

HOW SIMILAR ARE THEY?

Here are the numbers one to ten in Aymará, Quechua, and Spanish.

English	Aymará	Quechua	Spanish
one	ma	hoq	uno
two	payai	iskay	dos
three	quimsa	kinsa	tres
four	pusit	tawa	cuatro
five	pesca	pisqa	cinco
six	htaso	soqta	seis
seven	pakalkok	qanchis	siete
eight	quimsakalko	pusag	ocho
nine	yatun	isqon	nueve
ten	tunca	chunka	diez

The Jesuit missionary Ludovico Bertonio, who wrote the first Aymará-Spanish dictionary in 1610, described Aymará as a "genius of a language" because it is so well thought-out, with easy-to-understand linguistic rules.

QUECHUA Quechua was the language of the Incan Empire and, as a result, is still spoken by 13 million indigenous people in Peru, Bolivia, Ecuador, Chile, and northwest Argentina. This makes it an important international language. Because it covers such a wide area and so many different groups, Quechua has many different dialects. Some Quechua speakers would understand each other only with difficulty.

Recently scholars have come up with the idea of writing out common rules and vocabulary to unify the language. However, Quechua is largely an oral language with little written tradition, so this idea has not gone far.

AYMARÁ The Aymará people retained their language despite attempts to suppress it by both the Incas and the Spanish. Today it is spoken by about 2.5 million people in Peru, Bolivia, Argentina, and Chile. It is a harsh, guttural-sounding language, with sounds coming from the back of the throat.

It is said that 4,000 years ago a group of wise men sat down and made up the language from scratch. Since 1984 Aymará has been used in multilingual computerized translation. Iván Guzmán de Rojas, a Bolivian mathematician, created the computer program using Aymará as the intermediary language to translate European languages.

BEWARE THE FALSE FRIENDS

Many Spanish and English words look and sound the same. There are two reasons for this. Some words are similar because they originally came from the same Latin root. Other words have been borrowed from the other language. For example, Spanish has given the English language words such as *alligator, tomato, guitar, cork, armada*, and *vanilla*. A few words have even passed from Aymará or Quechua to Spanish, and from there to English. The best example of this is *llama* from Quechua.

Spanish also has many words that look the same as English words but have a different meaning. For example, *la carpeta* might be thought to mean "the carpet," but in fact it means "folder." *Jubilación* is not the Spanish word for "jubilation," but means "retirement." Such words are called false friends and are something people have to be aware of when learning Spanish.

A miner reads a Bolivian newspaper with a picture of elected president Evo Morales on the front page, January 22, 2006, in La Paz.

SPANISH

Spanish is one of the Romance languages, which means it originated from Latin. A version of vulgar Latin was first brought to Spain by Roman soldiers and settlers. Over the centuries it underwent many other influences until, by the Middle Ages, a distinctive Spanish language had emerged.

When the Spanish built up their huge colonial empire, they introduced their language to regions they conquered. As a result, about 350 million people around the world now speak Spanish as a first language, and businesspeople from Cuba, Bolivia, and Spain could quite happily communicate with each other in their common language. Spanish is also one of the official languages of the United Nations.

The Spanish spoken in Bolivian highlands is slower than what is heard in Spain, and most Bolivian people do not drop syllables as much. Some of the sounds are also different. The *z* and *ci* in words such as *manzana* and *gracias* are pronounced as a *th* sound in Spain but as an *s* sound in Bolivia.

The Bolivian Spanish has adopted many words from the Andean languages. Examples of Quechua words used by Spanish-speaking Bolivians include *wawa* (baby), *imilla* (girl), and *ilokalla* (boy).

NONVERBAL COMMUNICATION

Bolivian people of European background make great use of their hands when talking. They often make physical contact with each other, touching arms or shoulders to emphasize an important point.

The indigenous highland people are far less expressive. Even when arguing, they remain immobile and refrain from shouting. Instead, two people having the dispute talk simultaneously and continuously in a low, agitated voice.

When friends or acquaintances of Spanish background meet, it is very common for men to greet women, and women to greet other women, with a single kiss on the cheek. This is true for all ages and all occasions, and this European custom is spreading to other urban ethnic sectors. Two men meeting limit their contact to a handshake and maybe an embrace. Strangers do not kiss on the first meeting, but if they build a bond, they might kiss the next time they meet.

Indigenous people greeting each other are far more formal. At weddings or family gatherings, they shake hands and, at the same time, gently pat each other's shoulder with their free hand. They often lean forward as they do this, making it look as if they are about to kiss but then change their minds. Indigenous people shake hands very lightly.

Bolivian people are quite open about physical contact and expressing their affection. Men and women often walk down the street arm in arm. This is a particularly strong practice between fathers and daughters.

ARTS

BOLIVIA HAS A SURPRISINGLY diverse and rich culture. Music and dance are particularly strong, but Bolivian painters and sculptors have also produced some notable work. The National Academy of Fine Arts in La Paz promotes music, painting, sculpture, and ceramics.

Despite having a strong arts and literary scene, very few Bolivian writers or artists have attracted much attention outside the country. Many of these have only done so by moving overseas, particularly to the United States. One promising trend is that a number of high-profile artists, who fled during the military dictatorships, have returned to Bolivia.

Above: **A beautiful shawl, called a manta, woven by indigenous women. Many of them weave shawls both to wear and to sell to tourists to supplement the family income.**

Opposite: **An artist in a workshop painting a mask that will be used in festivals.**

Bolivia also has a rich heritage of folk art and handicrafts, which includes the costumes and masks created for fiestas. People often seek to identify links between contemporary Bolivian art and the traditional work of the indigenous population. Although the indigenous community has had some influence, particularly in music and dance, artists and writers have tended to be influenced more by their contemporaries in other Latin American countries.

Since World War II, the United States has also had an increasing influence on Bolivian art. With the arrival of satellite television, Bolivia's own culture might well have to compete against a great many more external influences in the years to come.

Dancing at the Santo Domingo festival in Achocalla.

There is a series of festival dances that the indigenous people created to make fun of the Spanish. In the past it was only at fiesta time that such "insolence" was tolerated by the colonialists, but now these dances have become part of the fiesta tradition.

DANCE

The folk dances that are performed today are a combination of pre-Hispanic dances, Spanish dances, and African dances brought to Bolivia by the slaves. One of the most famous, and the nearest Bolivia has to a national folk dance, is the *cueca* (KWAY-kah), or handkerchief dance. The *cueca* can trace its roots through the Chilean *cueca* to the Spanish fandango. The dance opens with an introduction, during which the partners look at each other provocatively, building up the tension. On the call of *adentro* (ah-DEN-troh), the couple starts to dance, partners whirling around each other, linking arms at times, and waving their handkerchiefs in spirals above their heads with their free hand. This stage of the dance symbolizes the man trying to win the woman, who escapes from him. During the second stage the dance becomes softer and gentler as the partners come to an agreement. The final stage of the dance is preceded by the cry of *zapateo!* (zah-pah-TAY-oh). This is a repeat of the first stage but with more force. At this point the spectators start clapping in time with the beat.

VISUAL ARTS

The Incas were magnificent artists, but their best work in gold and silver was melted down by the Spaniards. Modern Bolivian art started with the colonial period, and the first artwork was religious. The most renowned artist of that period was Melchor Pérez de Holguín, who was born in 1660. His religious paintings contain many strange touches. In one painting a saint talks to an angel, while in the background an alien-looking bird attacks a frog.

Church authorities employed mestizo artists, and in the 17th and 18th centuries a mestizo baroque style developed that mixed indigenous and Spanish styles.

The fathers of contemporary Bolivian art are Cecilio Guzmán de Rojas and Arturo Borda. Guzmán studied in Madrid, returning to Bolivia in 1929. He was one of the first painters to portray indigenous subjects, and Machu Picchu in Peru was a favorite theme. He also depicted the beauty and nobility of the indigenous Andean people. His style was influenced by cubism. On the other hand, Borda covered a wide range of subjects. A favorite was Mount Illimani, which he painted from all angles and in all different kinds of light.

Women artists have had much success in Bolivia too. María Núñez del Prado created sculptures from natural materials that were heavily influenced by the indigenous cultures. María Luisa Pacheco was a student of Guzmán but spent most of her career in the United States.

An easy way to begin appreciating modern Bolivian art would be to view the historic murals of Walter Solon Romero, often found in public buildings, especially in Sucre and La Paz. Edgar Arandia and Roberto Mamani Mamani take Bolivian art on two unique but colorful paths.

Typical folk painting of the Aymará.

TRADITIONAL MUSIC

Much of Bolivia's traditional music is based on simple instruments that boys play to pass the long hours while they are looking after the animals. As a result every village, even every street, usually has its own band.

Although the music and dance of the Altiplano are considered representative of Bolivia, in fact there is a remarkable degree of regional variation. The music of the cold, harsh Altiplano tends to be sad and mournful, but in the lowlands music is faster and more lively. Chaco music is the most distinctive and concentrates more on violin, drum, and guitar. This is largely due to the influence of Jesuit priests, who taught the indigenous peoples to play European instruments.

The most important recent trend is to introduce lyrics to the mournful Andean music, creating a new genre of folk songs. Folk musicians have the opportunity to play in street festivals, and the best groups might be invited to perform at a *peñas* (PAY-nyas). These are folk music shows that take place in restaurants.

Panpipes are a traditional instrument in Andean folk music.

Los Kjarkas is the best known of the Bolivian folk groups and plays a stylized kind of modern folk song. Other well-known groups include Savia Andina, popular for its poetic lyrics and love songs, and Wara, which has successfully combined traditional and modern music genres. Wara is also considered the best of the traditional Aymará groups.

Despite a growing influence from the Western music that is carried into the remotest homes by radio, traditional Bolivian folk music remains the most popular. Using authentic instruments, American musician Paul Simon recorded a version of the Andean folk song "El Condor Pasa," which has become a classic pop song in both Europe and North America.

MUSICAL INSTRUMENTS

Traditional Bolivian instruments generally come in families of small, large, and medium sizes. Most typical are the simple flutes made from reed pipes, which are known as *quenas* (KAY-nas), and the more complicated *zampoña* (zahm-POH-nya).

The *quena* (*above*) does not have a mouthpiece, but is played by blowing into a notch in the instrument. Traditionally it was a solo instrument, but it is now often incorporated into a musical ensemble. One recognized master of the reed flute is Gilbert Fabre.

Zampoñas, also known as panpipes, or by the Aymará name of *siku* (SEE-koo), are more complicated and consist of a collection of different-sized reeds lashed together. The sound is produced by forcing air across the open end of the reeds. It is the *zampoña* that gives Bolivian musical troupes much of their distinctive sound.

Shells and cow horns might also be used, and drums have also become a central part of Andes music, although many of the designs are based on Spanish military drums. String instruments include the *charango* (chah-RAN-goh), a small, guitarlike instrument with a high twangy sound. The *charango* was once made from an armadillo shell, but today, for ecological reasons, it is made of wood. Unlike the guitar, it has 10 strings arranged in pairs, and the best *churrangos* are prized works of art. Another string instrument is the *violin chapaco*, a variation of the European violin.

MODERN MUSIC

The Spanish had a major influence on South American music, including introducing the guitar, the piano, the military-style brass band, and the symphony orchestra. All these forms of music making are popular in Bolivia, particularly the brass bands that regularly play at indigenous weddings or religious occasions, or in parks and parades for people of all backgrounds.

Some of the numerous talented musicians produced by Bolivia include the great classical pianist Walter Ponce and violinist Jaime Laredo, winner of Belgium's Queen Elisabeth International Music Competition. Bolivia's Ana María Vera was the youngest pianist to be invited to perform at the Kennedy Center in Washington, D.C.

Alberto Villalpando is considered one of the country's leading contemporary composers. His music is inspired by Altiplano and traditional music, and he has composed an opera set in colonial Potosí. Fidel Torricos works with *cueca* and other popular dance music.

Some of the most popular musicians are *charango* players. The very best players, such as Mauro Núñez and his students Jaime Torres, Celestino Campos, and Ernesto Cavour, are famous throughout Bolivia.

The strength of Bolivia's musical tradition has made it harder for some forms of music to become accepted. Johnny González is a jazz singer with an international reputation, but he has had to struggle to get people to listen to him in his own country. After studying in the La Paz Conservatory, he went to France, where he played with Duke Ellington. Although González left Bolivia in the 1970s, he has recently been returning to his homeland to try to increase public interest in jazz. A newer generation of jazz fusion groups, such as Altiplano, Wara, and Bolivian Jazz, have an enthusiastic following in a few La Paz jazz clubs.

The National Symphony Orchestra has recently found new energy and is putting on many exciting programs under the guidance of the young conductor Freddy Terrazas. Terrazas is a good example of the talented artists who are returning to Bolivia.

A HOLLYWOOD MYTH TURNS TRUE

The most famous movie to feature Bolivia was *Butch Cassidy and the Sundance Kid*. The Hollywood hit starred Paul Newman and Robert Redford and followed the path of two outlaws who flee from the United States to Bolivia. The movie was based on a well-known piece of western folklore, but nobody was sure what was accurate and what was legend.

However, historians have hunted through old Bolivian mining records and discovered that in 1908 there indeed was a series of robberies by two North American bandits. Local people knew where the graves of the two bandits were supposed to be and led investigators to the spot. When the investigators dug, they found two skeletons. The DNA tests were inconclusive, but the search goes on.

Rock music is popular in Bolivia, especially among youth. The movement includes groups such as Wara, Octavia, and more recently Atajo or Camaleón. One trend is to combine rock with folk music.

MOVIES

In the 1960s and 1970s Bolivian movies came to international attention with the work of two major directors, Antonio Eguino and Jorge Sanjinés. This was the period of "militant cinema," when movies looked at Bolivia's problems, particularly the plight of the indigenous people. Sanjinés's most famous movie is perhaps *Yawar Mallku* (*Blood of the Condor*), a chilling story of American doctors who sterilize indigenous women who come to their clinic. One of Eguino's best known movies is *Chuquiago*, which follows four overlapping stories in different social classes in La Paz.

Because of the way the cinema has championed the cause of the nation's poor and highlighted problems in the social system, military governments have often cracked down on the movie industry, and Sanjinés himself has spent several years in exile.

By the end of the twentieth century Bolivian cinema had become even more active. Sanjinés has produced *La Nación Clandestina* (*The Clandestine Nation*), which tells the story of an Aymará man's life in the city. *Cuestión de Fe* (*A Question of Faith*), a road comedy directed by Marcos Loayza, won many awards around the world. More recently, *Di Buen Día a Papá* (*Say Good Morning to Dad*), directed by Fernando Vargas, tells the story of a family living in the region where Che Guevara was executed.

LITERATURE

For many experts Gabriel René-Moreno (1836–1908) left a wonderful description of life in early Bolivia in spite of an overly procolonial view. Franz Tamayo, who lived between 1879 and 1956, was the first writer to champion the cause of the indigenous population. Particularly in his poems, he described the nobility of these people, a most unusual view at the time for an aristocrat. In 1935 Tamayo was elected president, but a coup prevented him from taking office.

Another writer to take up the rights of the indigenous population was Alcides Arguedas, a sociologist and diplomat, who was born in the same year as Tamayo. Arguedas's main novels, *Wata Wara* and *Raza de Bronce*, brought him fame throughout Latin America. Jesús Lara, who wrote about indigenous peasant life, is one of the few Bolivian authors to be widely read outside the country.

The most outstanding modern author is José Wolfango Montes Vannuci who, in 1987, published his highly acclaimed novel *Jonah and the Pink Whale*. This is a very funny account of life in the boomtown of Santa Cruz. This novel was later made into a movie.

It is important to know that books are very expensive in Bolivia. With most Bolivians earning low wages, and the lack of facilities like public libraries, people are forced to buy used or pirated books if they want to read at all.

FOLK ART

It is said that in Bolivia the best art is not found in museums but on the streets. There is certainly a rich heritage of folk art, particularly weaving. Bolivian weaving is considered to be of a particularly high quality. First the wool is spun on a small spindle into a single strand. It is then transferred to a larger spindle and spun into a two-ply yarn. After being dyed it is given a third spin. It is this third spin that gives Bolivian cloth its strength, elasticity, and hard, smooth surface.

Indigenous women spend long hours spinning or weaving on rigid heddle looms, and the textiles they produce come in many varied styles and patterns, with considerable regional influences. The best textiles are generally considered to be the red and black designs from the town of Potolo. One modern influence is the increased use of the less expensive sheeps' wool rather than that of llama and alpaca.

Other well-developed forms of folk art include musical instruments, particularly the *charango*, masks, and silver jewelry.

A BOLIVIAN VILLAGE TAKES ON THE ART DEALERS

Throughout their history the Aymará have woven beautiful textiles in vibrant colors. The oldest and finest cloths came from Coroma, where the people believed the fabrics contained the souls of their ancestors. The beautiful pieces were only brought out on the Day of the Dead. Many of the cloths were later stolen by Bolivians, who sold them to rich collectors in the United States.

There did not seem to be any way that a poor remote Bolivian village could take on the rich New York art dealers, but thanks to wide publicity and support from groups in the United States, a formal agreement allowed for the return of the stolen textiles to the Bolivian village. Although this agreement expired in 1996, the United States and Bolivia signed another agreement in 2001 that imposes import restrictions on pre-Columbian archaeological artifacts and colonial and Republican ethnological materials.

LEISURE

HOLIDAYS AND WEEKENDS IN BOLIVIA are a time to spend with friends and family, reinforcing ties and bonds and enjoying each other's company. On special occasions such as weddings or festivals, family gatherings involve a considerable amount of singing, dancing, and feasting. At other times, such as on a quiet weekend, time together is more likely to be spent lingering over a leisurely meal with the traditional conversation hour afterward.

Above: **A child feeding pigeons in La Paz.**

Opposite: **Two indigenous women shaking hands and shopping in a market in La Paz.**

In cities, public parks form an important part of social life. The park is a place where children play soccer and ride their bikes. Adults sit in the sun talking, and teenage couples cuddle together on benches, oblivious to everybody around them. Generally when adults sit in the park, they seem happy enough just to pass the time in conversation, but groups of men might play cards or dice.

Many people belong to special dance clubs that devote months practicing to perform at major festivals. Members of dance teams might spend several hundred dollars on their elaborate costumes.

For indigenous women, free time is largely spent knitting or weaving. Partly this might be considered work because many of the items they make will be sold for extra income. However, the women feel a great deal of pleasure and pride from their handicraft.

When children spin tops, they probably do not realize that they are playing a game that has been enjoyed in Bolivia since Incan times, when it was known as *pisqoynyo* (pees-COIN-yo).

CHILDREN'S GAMES

Many Bolivian children have little money to spend on toys, so they have to improvise their own games or make their own toys with what materials they can find. An old bicycle wheel will become a hoop, a pile of stones building bricks.

The most popular game of all is spinning tops, and small wooden tops are for sale in every market. The game is usually played by boys from the ages of 7 or 8 through the early teenage years. Most boys like to spin the top and then slide two fingers underneath it and try to pick it up while it is still spinning. Once the top is in their hand, they will try to drop it onto an upturned bottle cap.

Marbles, using factory-made glass marbles, is another popular game. The players each place a marble in a circle drawn in the dirt. Taking turns, they then flick a second marble into the arena. From this point on, players win any marble they hit with their marble. Although seemingly simple, the game has many additional rules that the boys playing all seem to understand.

Other common street games include clapping games, chase games, and games played with stones, where players try to throw their stones as close to a mark on the ground as possible.

In the rural areas, slingshots made from forked tree branches and old elastic strips are popular. This game allows boys to practice their skill and is useful in scaring birds off the crops.

Some villages arrange bullfights. These are not the Spanish type of bullfight but rather are staged between two prized bulls that are brought together in an open field. After much pawing of the ground, the two animals lock horns in battle, to the delight of the cheering crowd, who are generally sensible enough to keep a fair distance away.

TRADITIONAL SPORTS

Apart from soccer, which is played nearly everywhere, sports are largely enjoyed by the urban population. For the majority of Bolivians in the countryside, life is simply too hard to leave them with much energy or enthusiasm for sports.

Bolivia does have a few traditions that could be considered sports. *Tinku* (TEEN-koo), which takes place on rural highland festival days, is a bare-fisted type of boxing that starts off as a highly ritualistic dance and usually breaks down into a free-for-all in which the contestants try to knock each other down by any means possible. Fists and feet fly, and the whole event is a great favorite with crowds. Indeed, as people get more and more excited, the violence often spills over into the audience. This modern version is tame compared with earlier versions, when the boys taking part used slings to throw cacti at each other.

There is also a yearly swimming race across the narrowest part of Lake Titicaca. The distance is not particularly long, but the water is extremely cold, making it a test of endurance for the competitors. Another annual event limited to those with mythical stamina is the La Paz marathon, held at 12,000 feet (3,660 m) above sea level, with some of the most grueling uphill terrain known in the sport.

A NATION OF SOCCER LOVERS

Soccer is the national sport of Bolivia and is played everywhere, from parks to the street. Supporters show their loyalty to the best teams by placing stickers in their cars or by wearing replicas of their favorite team's shirts.

Important games are played at the national stadium in La Paz, where the home team always has a great advantage because of the altitude. As a result, Bolivia has won many of its international games. The most notable occasion came in 1963, when the national team won the South American Championship in their own high-altitude stadium.

A neighborhood soccer game. Soccer is very popular in Bolivia, both to play and to watch. In one village everyone had gathered around the television to watch a World Cup game and was so engrossed in the match that no one noticed that a fire had broken out until half the number of houses in the village had burned down!

In the 1994 World Cup qualifying tournament, the Bolivian team notched up a whole series of good results. They beat Brazil 2-0, Uruguay 3-1, and then traveled to Venezuela, where they hit seven goals past the home team. These victories helped Bolivia become one of the 24 nations to qualify for the World Cup finals in the United States. They did not win there, but just getting to the World Cup was a great achievement.

Bolivia hosted the 1997 South American Championship. This caused a polemic since some of the games were to be played in La Paz, which, according to rival teams, favored the Bolivians due to the altitude of the city. The French president came to Bolivia's defense, and the Fédération Internationale de Football Association (FIFA) had to accept that games be played in La Paz. Even though Bolivia made it to the finals, they did not win the championship against Brazil. Since then, Bolivia has not had a very successful team.

Bolivia has a professional league for their strongest clubs. Traditionally the best teams are Jorge Wilstermann, Bolívar, and The Strongest. But teams from the lowlands, such as Blooming and Oriente Petrolero, receive sponsorship from the oil companies and are able to attract some of the best players.

Soccer is not just a game for professional players. Hundreds of men, but very few women, play soccer for recreation. The better players may belong to local teams that have team uniforms and play on full-sized fields, although they will generally be fields of mud or sand rather than grass. Less serious players join casual games in the park. These games are usually played on a concrete arena the size of a basketball court, with four or five players on each team. The games end when the first goal is scored, the winners staying to play the next opponents.

The star Bolivian soccer player Marco Antonio Etcheverry, known as El Diablo, played for a top club in Chile. He is famous both for his skill and his wild temper. Etcheverry has played in the U.S. Major League Soccer (MLS) team D.C. United and has now retired.

THE WORLD'S MOST FAMOUS SOCCER SCHOOL

In 1978 businessman Rolando Aguilera Pareja had the idea of opening up a soccer school for the poor children of the city of Santa Cruz. On the first day 250 children arrived at the gate of Tahuichi Academy, and since then, 150,000 have benefited from the academy's work.

Tahuichi's best teams have won youth tournaments all over the world, and over 60 of their graduates now play for professional clubs. However, Tahuichi Academy has always been primarily interested in the children themselves, and soccer is merely a tool to give them pride and a purpose in life. The academy therefore also oversees the children's health, nutrition, and education.

The spectacular ski resort at Chacaltaya is so high up that visiting skiers often have to ski with oxygen bottles strapped to their backs.

OTHER SPORTS

Bolivians play many different sports, and every four years they send a small team to the Olympic Games. However, they have yet to win a medal. In the Pan American Games, held between all nations of the Americas, Bolivia has won a total of three medals—one silver and two bronze. In the 2002 South American Games, Bolivia won nine bronze medals, but no titles. Only the tiny country of Surinam ranked below Bolivia at the medals table.

Basketball is the second most popular sport, followed by volleyball, and there are nationwide league competitions for both sports.

Wealthy people are likely to try sailing or golf. La Paz has the highest golf course in the world. Because of the thin air, players find they can hit the ball longer distances than at sea level. Tennis and racquets are also popular. The latest craze with the rich Bolivians is motor sports, particularly go-carts and motorbike racing. Some of the world's toughest long-distance rallye races pass through Bolivia.

The Bolivian Andes offer some of the most spectacular mountain climbing in the world. The king of Bolivian mountain climbing is Bernardo Guarachi. He has been to the top of Illimani more than 170 times and has traveled around the world climbing the great peaks, including Mount Everest. He is often called on to make rescue climbs and once carried an injured climber down from the mountain on his back.

Gravity-assisted cycling is another breathtaking sport, especially enjoyed by tourists. Starting in the cold mountains and wheeling downhill around scary hairpin turns, swerving away from the deep gorges, cyclists will reach the hot lowlands after six hours of fright and delight.

SHOESHINE BOYS

Shoeshine boys are seen everywhere in Bolivian towns. Most are young boys, starting at 6 or 7 years-old, but old men also provide this service. Some have permanent chairs, almost like thrones, on which customers climb up, sit, and have their shoes polished while they read the newspaper. Other shoeshine boys carry all their equipment with them in small boxes and wait around park benches for customers.

Now shoeshine boys are expanding their business. They carry cell phones and the customer can make a call on them for 15 cents.

For some observers, shoeshine boys seem like an innocuous part of the landscape, but others consider this as child labor. Boys who have not dropped out of school often wear masks to avoid being identified by their schoolmates. Many give most of their earnings to their underemployed parents. But some are homeless, sniff glue, and sleep on the streets.

WEEKENDS

Friday night is a popular time to go out on the town. One traditional Friday night activity, mainly among some middle-class men, is known as *viernes de soltero* (VYAIR-nays day sohl-TAY-roh), or single man's Friday, when even married men pretend they are single for the night and drink and play dice or cards. Many of their wives go out with each other rather than sit at home waiting for their husbands.

Bolivians of all ages and all social classes love to dance. Sometimes they partner across age lines in family gatherings or else join peer groups or schoolmates. The excuse for such get-togethers is often a birthday or traditional celebration. Sunday afternoons are usually reserved for family gatherings and barbecues, while various cities open their downtowns as strolling areas.

In the cities there are also cultural activities such as concerts and art expositions. Some people like to get together in intellectual cafés and debate on various subjects.

FESTIVALS

FESTIVALS PLAY A MAJOR PART in Bolivian culture. There are ancient festivals that go back to Incan times and religious celebrations that are the legacy of centuries of Spanish rule. At fiesta time the two cultures often become interwoven, with older Incan ceremonies being incorporated into modern religious celebrations.

Some fiestas are celebrated throughout the country, and others are regional. Each department has its own public holiday, and most towns and villages have a festival for their special patron saint. There are other events that take place several times a year or even weekly. The Copacabana car-blessing ceremony by priests is a good example of a weekly celebration.

Fiestas are an important part of religious life and are major social occasions that bind communities together. Influential individuals who sponsor the fiestas often do so to secure their own position in society and build on their power and prestige.

Bolivians are usually happy to celebrate, whatever the occasion, and festivals quickly turn into colorful parties with street parades, dance, music, fireworks, craft sales, games, piñatas, feasting, and drinking. Another activity that adds to the fun during the pre-Lent carnival is when young men throw water bombs—balloons filled with water—at each other and anybody else who happens to be nearby.

For most people, fiestas give an important two- or three-day break from the daily routine. Indeed, in the past, it was possibly only the chewing of coca and the thought of another festival that enabled the working class population to endure their difficult conditions.

Above: **A girl dresses as the queen of the Tarabuco Phujllay Festival.**

Opposite: **Girls in Oruro celebrate a weeklong carnival in November after All Saints' Day with music, dance, and elaborate costumes.**

EL GRAN PODER

El Gran Poder (el grahn poh-DAIR) is a recent festival that started as a simple candlelit procession through the streets of La Paz in 1939. Since then, El Gran Poder has grown to become today's great street parade.

Celebrated around end May or early June, the parade goes for 8 miles (13 km) around the streets of La Paz, testing the stamina of the dancers and marching bands, and delighting the crowds of people, who come from all over the world. The range of costumes is magnificent and reflects every aspect of Bolivian history and mythology. The most famous dancers are Los Morenos (los moh-RAY-nohs), whose costumes represent Africans.

FIESTA DEL ESPÍRITU

The Fiesta del espíritu is rooted in the mining traditions of Potosí. It is an occasion for the miners to make an offering to Pachamama, the earth mother, in the hope that she will protect them. The festival is staged on the last three Saturdays in June, and then again in August.

In the days leading up to the festival, villagers bring llamas into town, until the streets look like one great animal market. Each mine selects one of their workers to buy a llama for their mine. The purchases take place on the morning of the festival and are followed by an hour or so of drinking and chewing coca. At midday the llamas are sacrificed. Some of the blood is caught and thrown down the mine, and later the stomach, feet, and head are buried as a further offering. After the sacrifice the men return to their drinking while the women prepare the llama meat for the feast that follows.

ALASITAS FESTIVAL

Alasitas (ah-lah-SEE-tahs), or the festival of abundance, is an Aymará festival that takes place in La Paz and around Lake Titicaca. It is held on different dates in different towns, but in the capital it takes place on January 24. Originally Alasitas was held to ensure a good crop and was staged in September, which is the Bolivian spring. The Spanish moved the festival to January.

Ekekos with accessories. Ekeko's gifts are no longer limited to a good crop but might include money, a house, and a car. When people present Ekeko with money, they usually give him copies of U.S. dollars rather than bolivianos.

The festival centers around Ekeko, the god of the household and possessions. On the festival day there is a whole street of stalls selling models of Ekeko and tiny accessories that people can buy for him. These represent all the things people wish to receive themselves.

It is thought to bring good luck to buy these items at exactly noon, which means there is a terrible rush with everybody pushing and shoving. It is also considered to be luckier still to have the items given to you by a friend than to buy them yourself.

COSTUMES AND MASKS

Costumes are a particularly important feature of any fiesta, and a whole folk art has developed around making costumes and masks. These change yearly, with new ideas incorporated all the time. A famous costume maker was once asked why he added dragons to the devil's mask, and he replied that he had seen them in a Chinese movie! The major parades are now televised, so a new costume that appears in La Paz might be used in Oruro a few months later. A general trend has been for the work to become more dramatic in design but, sadly, less carefully made.

People not directly involved dress up in their best clothes, and even the poorest farmer usually owns a dark Western-style suit that is set aside for festival days. As always, indigenous women prefer traditional dress and put on layer after layer of their most colorful underskirts and wear their best embroidered shawls.

Los Morenos In their costumes with raised embroidery with silver threads, Los Morenos (lohs moh-RAY-nohs) dancers look almost like robots from a science fiction movie. With their exaggerated lips and teeth, they represent the African slaves. *Matracas* (mah-TRAH-kahs), a kind of rattle, are an important feature of Los Morenos's dance. The rattles come in all sorts of designs, sometimes with models of tractors, footballs, or even computers fixed onto them. Since about 1990 women have been allowed to dance alongside Los Morenos in the parade.

Auki-Auki Auki-Auki (OW-kee OW-kee) dancers represent old colonial men. They wear a cloak, but their main feature is the mask with its long pointed nose and an oversized top hat. This is covered with streamers that run down the back. The costume is completed by a long white beard and a twisted cane.

Devils The famous devils from the Oruro Festival wear white or red bodysuits with gloves and boots in the same color. They have a heavily embroidered breastplate and a belt made up of hundreds of coins. Their masks (*left*) are the most dramatic feature and have bulging eyes and elaborate horns.

Animals Many dancers dress as animals, particularly bears and condors. The bear costume consists of a fur bodysuit, usually brown or black, often with a white chest. The mask is large and ferocious, and the teeth might be made from mirrors to catch the sunlight.

Angels The angels wear white clothing with colored tights and a pink mask. The boots and other trimming are often sky blue. They wear silver helmets and carry a small shield and a sword, making them look almost like European knights in armor. Wings are sometimes attached to the costume.

ORURO FESTIVAL

The largest carnivals are generally those staged in February and March, in the weeks leading up to Lent. All major Bolivian towns stage weeklong festivals at this time, but the largest and most famous is *la diablada*, the dance of the devil, which takes place in the mining town of Oruro.

The festival is based on local folklore. Legend tells that the Virgin of Candelaria took pity on a thief who had been mortally wounded in a robbery and helped him home so he could die in his own village. The next morning the local people found his body draped over a statue of the Virgin.

The grand parade takes part on the opening day of the festival. First come the cars and trucks decorated with jewelry, coins, and silver. Then come the dance troupes led by the Archangel Michael, dressed in sky blue and carrying his sword and shield. He is followed by people dressed as bears, condors, and devils. The devil figures wear the biggest masks of all. These are carved with horns and serpents, and sometimes even have bulging flashing lights for eyes. After that there are marchers dressed as Incas, Kallawaya medicine men, dancers with headdresses of tropical feathers, conquistadores, and miners carrying gifts for El Tío (the devil).

Young Bolivians getting a condor ready for the parade at the Oruro festival.

The parade finishes at the stadium, where the *diablada* takes place. *Supay* (SOO-pay), an evil spirit believed to live in the center of the earth, fights Saint Michael in a ritual dance, in which the forces of good triumph over evil.

On May 18, 2001, UNESCO declared the Oruro Festival one of the "Masterpieces of the Oral and Intangible Heritage of Humanity."

CHRISTMAS

In urban areas Christmas is celebrated in much the same way as in the United States. Celebrations in the countryside have more to do with farming and the seasons and are really a continuation of the Incan Festival of the Sun. At this time of year the crops have just been planted and the llamas have given birth, so life on the earth is very vulnerable. The Aymará used to make little clay models of each of their animals at this time to bring good luck, but this tradition has been largely forgotten. Aymará people attend church on Christmas but do not give gifts.

Until recently, groups of children who dressed in costumes or just put on ponchos walked around the streets singing *villancicos* (vee-yan-SEE-kos), Christmas carols, and playing drums and other instruments. It was traditional to give the children small gifts of food or money.

The main Christmas decoration in the home has always been a nativity scene. From December 15 whole streets are lined with market stalls selling polystyrene grottoes and plaster figures to place in them.

On Christmas Eve some families attend midnight Mass, and then relatives go back to one house together. When they arrive, in the early hours of Christmas day, they have the main Christmas meal of *picana* (pee-CAH-nah). This is a stew with chicken, beef, pork, various vegetables, including chunks of corn and potatoes, and wine or beer. Dessert is custard flan or *pandulce* (pahn-DOOL-say), a bread with nuts and raisins. After the meal family members exchange presents. At two or three in the morning they go to bed.

Stores in **La Paz** put on more elaborate Christmas displays each year, and men dressed as Santa Claus sometimes appear outside the shops.

Bolivia's National Day, on August 6, is celebrated with a parade.

OTHER HOLIDAYS

NEW YEAR'S The new year is celebrated with one great party. Generally families gather at one house and see the new year in together. After midnight the younger people might go to a nightclub while the older family members continue the party at home.

On these occasions the host family provides food, but it is common for everyone to pay something toward the cost. As at Christmas *picana* is the main meal, a pork stew called *fricasé* (FREE-kah-say) is served very early in the morning. *Fricasé* is said to be particularly good for partygoers who have drunk too much! After that people drift home to sleep.

An increasingly common alternative for wealthy people is to attend an organized New Year's celebration at their sports or social club.

HISTORIC AND POLITICAL HOLIDAYS Bolivia also has several holidays that celebrate important historic and political anniversaries. Labor Day is on May 1. Most people who work in labor and activist organizations gather for meetings and speeches, and organized marches are launched. This is in fact a holiday celebrated around the world as a day of protest. Ironically, May 1 is no longer a holiday in the country where it originated, in the United States, although Labor Day is celebrated on the first Monday in September.

Discovery of America Day is on October 12. This used to be a holiday, but the 500th anniversary celebration became a controversial issue in Bolivia. Indigenous Bolivians protested that their ancestors had been in America for hundreds of years before Columbus arrived. The government thus abandoned the holiday.

FESTIVALS CALENDAR

JANUARY
Kings' Day. Celebrates the day the three wise men visited Baby Jesus.
Alasitas Festival. Dedicated to Ekeko. The main celebration is in La Paz.

FEBRUARY
Fiesta of the Virgin of Candelaria. Celebrated in several towns, although the main event is in Copacabana.
La Diablada Carnival. Great street parade followed by the devil's dance in Oruro. The largest and most famous of a nationwide series of pre-Lent carnivals.
Oruro Festival. Large carnivals are held during the weeks leading to Lent.

MARCH
Fiesta de la Uva. A grape festival in Tarija.
Phujllay. A very dramatic festival staged in Tarabuco, near Sucre. Dancers and musicians celebrate the Battle of Lumbati.

MARCH–APRIL
Easter. Observed throughout the country.

MAY
Festival of the Cross. Celebrations in various Bolivian towns, most notably in Tarija, where the festival lasts nearly two weeks.
Mother's Day. Commemorated nationwide, but particularly important in Cochabamba, where the women of the town once defended the city from Spanish troops.

JUNE
Festival of the Holy Trinity. Takes place in the city of Trinidad. Bull-riding competitions are featured.
Fiesta del Espíritu. Takes place on the last three Saturdays of the month and again in August. This is a time when miners offer sacrifices to the pagan earth mother in exchange for protection.

San Juan Midyear Festival. Staged at the height of the cold months. People play with fireworks and light fires on the hillside or in the doorway of their houses, leaping over the flames to bring good luck. The fires also represent the warmer months that lie ahead.

JULY
Fiesta del Santo Patrono de Moxos. A major festival in the village of San Ignacio de Moxos. The festival is famous for its wild dancing.
Fiesta de Nuestra Señora del Carmen. Also known as Day of La Paz. A religious celebration merging with a cultural and tourism fair.

AUGUST
National Day. Celebrations take place throughout the country on August 6.
Festival of the Virgin of Urkupiña. Staged in the town of Quillacollo, this is the largest festival in Cochabamba.

SEPTEMBER
Festival of San Roque. Mainly a Tarija event in honor of Saint Roque. He is the patron saint of dogs, and this is reflected in the costumes.

OCTOBER
Festival of the Virgin of Rosario. Festivals take place in many Bolivian towns.

NOVEMBER
All Saints' Day. On November 1 and 2, Bolivians visit the graves of their relatives.

DECEMBER
Christmas. Celebrated throughout Bolivia.

FOOD

MEALS IN BOLIVIA ARE based on a great many recipes for but a few staple foods. There is considerable regional variety, but wherever one is, meat is likely to form the central part of the diet and is usually served with rice or potatoes and sometimes both.

Bread also plays a large part in the Bolivian diet. Bolivia grows wheat around Santa Cruz and also receives grain from the United States. There are bread sellers on every street corner, and the price is subsidized by the government.

Diet is influenced by the region people live in and their income. Potatoes are the staple food in the highlands, but in the lowlands they are largely replaced by rice, plantain, and yucca. A family in the Altiplano generally has less access to vegetables and fruit than a family living in the lowlands. Middle-class families have far greater variety in their diet.

The style and taste of bread varies from city to city, but in La Paz, marraquetas (marr-ah-KEH-tahs), which look like miniature French loaves, are the most popular.

Left: **A street stall offers a wide range of snacks.**

Opposite: **A street vendor selling fresh produce in La Paz.**

Selling potatoes at the market in Cochabamba. There are many different kinds of potatoes in the Andes, including yellow and purple varieties.

Llama meat is seldom eaten by middle-class people, who consider it inferior to beef. However, llama meat is lower in fat and might well be healthier to consume than beef.

POTATOES AND OTHER TUBERS

Potatoes and other tuberous plants make up a major part of the Bolivian diet. Potatoes come in various sizes and colors, with claims of two or three hundred different varieties being grown in different regions.

Potatoes originated in the Americas and were being eaten by the indigenous people there long before the Spanish arrived. The early conquistadores took potatoes back to Spain and from there their popularity spread throughout northern Europe and the British Isles.

In addition to potatoes, people eat a large number of other kinds of tuberous plants, including *oca* and *anu*. *Oca* is a fleshy root that grows between 2 to 4 inches (5 to 10 cm) long. It looks like a pink sausage and can be boiled, roasted, or fried. *Anu* is a yellow-white plant that looks and tastes similar to a parsnip. Two other basic foods that are widely eaten are *choclo* (CHOH-kloh), which is a large type of corn, and *habas* beans. *Habas* beans are collected from the wild and are either roasted or put in stews.

THE MEAL PATTERN

Breakfast is called *desayuno* (day-sie-OO-noh) and is quite simple, frequently little more than a roll with coffee. Children usually eat bread and either jelly and butter, or cheese, and drink milk with cocoa or drops of coffee. People rushing to work might stop to buy a bowl of chicken soup from a street vendor.

In cities, lunch, or *almuerzo* (al-MWER-zoh), is the most important meal of the day. Many restaurants offer a set lunch, including an appetizer, soup, a beef or chicken dish, and dessert. These are very popular and cost as little as 80 cents. Lunch is a leisurely occasion, even on workdays, and it is not unusual to see businessmen linger over coffee in no apparent rush to get back to work.

On weekends, lunch with family and friends becomes a major social event and can last for a while. At the end of the meal, coffee, tea, or *maté* (MAH-tay), a drink made of plant and flower extractions, is served at the table. Then people move to the garden and resume their conversations. This is known as *sobremesa* (soh-bray-MAY-sah), or the after-lunch hour. Frequently a guest invited for lunch is still there when the evening meal is served.

In rural areas the meal pattern is very different. Altiplano farmers have only two meals a day; the first eaten early in the morning, and the second in the evening after work. The diet in these communities is monotonous, with the basic meal made up of quinoa, *oca*, and potatoes. Indigenous families usually eat outside if it is not raining. The men, particularly, do not feel comfortable eating openly in front of strangers, so when they are away from home, they usually face a wall when they are eating and sit hunched over their food.

In the countryside, cooking is either done indoors, using a large metal pot suspended over a fire, or outdoors on small clay stoves fueled with reeds or whatever else is available locally.

Quinoa is a local grain that is high in protein. It can be ground into flour or used to thicken porridge dishes and stews.

125

FAVORITE RECIPES

Most Bolivian recipes have meat in them, and beef, chicken, and fish are popular with people who can afford them. Poorer people generally have to be content with lamb, goat, or llama meat.

One of the most common dinners is *silpancho* (seel-PAN-choh), which is pounded beef with an egg cooked on top. Soups, stews, and broth are very popular in Bolivia. Lamb is often served this way in meals such as *thimpu* (TEEM-poo), which is a spicy stew cooked with vegetables. *Saice* (SIE-say) is another meaty broth, and *fricasé* is a pork stew seasoned with yellow *ají* (a-HEE), or hot pepper.

Hot, spicy sauces are popular additions to any dish. These might be made from tomatoes or pepper pods and are usually placed on the table in a small dish so that people can add as much or as little as they wish.

The lowlands diet includes the meat of many wild animals, particularly armadillo, which are commonly found in the woodlands.

CHUÑO OR FREEZE-DRIED POTATOES

Indigenous groups living on the Altiplano have their own way of freeze-drying potatoes and *oca* so that they turn into *chuño* (CHOO-nyoh). Any surplus crop is spread on the ground to freeze at night and then allowed to thaw in the sunlight.

For several days in a row the vegetables are trampled with bare feet to squeeze out the moisture. This finally leaves a light, dry husk that can be stored for months.

Chuño can be added to stews and soups, and travelers take it on journeys because it rehydrates and cooks quickly.

FRUITS AND DESSERTS

Bolivia has an excellent selection of fruits. These include several fruits that are not easily found in the United States: custard apples, prickly pear cactus, passion fruit, and a range of mangos. These have become available recently in some areas, however.

Desserts with a local flavor include *tojori* (toh-HOH-ree) and *thaya* (TIE-ah). With the consistency of porridge, *tojori* is made from corn, cinnamon, and sugar all mashed together. *Thaya* are a favorite on the Altiplano and are made from apple puree mixed with sugared water and spiced with cinnamon and cloves. This mixture is shaped into little domes and placed on the roofs of houses to freeze overnight. In the morning a little sugar water colored with local spices is added. The town of Potosí specializes in pastries, including *tawa-tawas*, which are deep-fried pastries served in syrup.

A special dessert saved for festivals are *confites* (kohn-FEE-tays), which are made by local confectioners and sold on festival days. They are made from boiled sugar syrup hardened around nuts, aniseed, fruit, biscuits, or coconuts, and they come in an amazing variety of colors.

Bolivia has many varieties of bananas, some of which are used for cooking. Bananas baked in their skins are a favorite dessert or snack.

EXCELLENT CHEESES

Bolivia has a wide range of cheeses, many of which are excellent. On the Altiplano, cheese made from sheep's milk is the most common. It is a slightly soft cheese, almost like a French brie, and it has a rather strong smell that some people dislike. Middle-class Bolivians seem to prefer the more expensive cheeses made from cow's milk. The best Bolivian cheeses are generally thought to be those from Tarija city. Tarija hosts the Festival of Wine and Cheese every year.

Salteñas for sale from a street vendor.

STREET FOOD

In the cities the favorite snack is the *salteña* (sal-TAY-nyah). These little oval pies are eaten as a quick lunch or a tasty and filling snack. *Salteñas* are stuffed with chicken or beef and whatever else is available. This might include different vegetables, such as potatoes and onions, and eggs. The final touch is a big helping of spices to give the pies their distinctive taste. *Salteñas* are the subject of considerable debate, and everyone seems to know one shop or stall that bakes the very best in town.

Empanadas (em-pah-NAH-dahs) are filled with either beef, chicken, or cheese. They can be baked in bread or deep-fried in fat. Another fast food specialty is *humintas* (oo-MEEN-tahs). These are made from cornmeal with various additional fillings, shaped into a triangle, and wrapped in a corn husk. Like *salteñas*, they come in many different varieties.

Bolivia's traditional fast foods are coming under considerable competition from hamburgers and french fries. In the big cities these are sold from little kiosks on almost every street and are extremely popular.

DRINKS

Black tea is probably the most common Bolivian drink. It is served strong, with lots of sugar. *Maté de coca* (MAH-tay day KOH-kah), which is tea with coca leaves added, is also very popular and is said to be a good cure for altitude sickness.

Refresco (ray-FRES-koh) is a fruit juice with a dried peach in the bottom of the glass. *Tostada* (tohs-TA-da) is made from a combination of barley, honey, cinnamon, cloves, and water. These are mixed in plastic containers and poured into glasses lined up for thirsty customers. A metal saucer is placed on top to keep the dirt and dust out.

Chicha is a potent, homemade corn beer that has been brewed since Incan times and probably for hundreds of years before then. To make *chicha*, women chew corn into small balls called *muko* (MOO-koh) and leave them to dry in the sun. The *muko* are then boiled with chunks of meat, grain, and sugar. Spices give a regional flavor to each brew. Local people know which houses *chicha* is brewed in, and on festival days people walk around the streets selling it by the glass.

There is also a drink called *singani* (seen-GAH-nee) that is made from grapes and is a cross between whiskey and wine.

Men drinking *chicha* in a *chicha* house in Cochabamba.

TEATIME

Though late afternoon teatime is mainly thought of as a British tradition, it became a custom in Bolivia, imported by British miners. It used to be specific to the highlands and often among well-to-do people, but this custom has spread to different regions and social classes. Teatime is often an occasion to invite friends or family. Poorer people eat bread alone with their tea. Those who can afford it will have pastries, cheese, butter, and jelly.

FRICASÉ (HOT AND SPICY PORK STEW)

2 pounds (0.9 kg) of boneless pork
2 medium-sized onions
2 teaspoons of yellow (or red) chili powder or paprika powder
2 teaspoons of cumin
6 cloves of garlic
1 can of hominy (alternative: 6 or 8 medium sized potatoes, boiled separately)
1 teaspoon of salt (optional)
4–6 cups of cold water

This stew is ideal for a cold winter day. Cut the pork in chunks of about 2 or 3 inches (5 or 8 cm) in size. If the pork is lean, add two teaspoons of oil when cooking it. Dice the onions and garlic. Put everything, except the hominy or potatoes, in a pot and bring it to a boil.

Lower the heat and simmer until the meat turns tender (about 40 to 60 minutes). Add the hominy or potatoes and let it boil for another 2 or 3 minutes.

Serve the stew warm. This recipe serves six to eight people.

COMPOTA DE DURAZNO (PEACH COMPOTE)

1 dozen fresh medium-sized whole peaches
4 tablespoons of natural brown sugar
1 teaspoon of cinnamon
1 tablespoon of cornstarch
3 cups of water

Wash the peaches and peel them. Put the skinned peaches into a pot with the water and add the cinnamon and sugar. Boil it on medium heat until the peaches are tender. Combine the cornstarch with a little water, then lower the flame and add the cornstarch gradually while stirring until it partially thickens. Let it cool down. Serve the dessert when it has cooled. This recipe is sufficient for six servings.

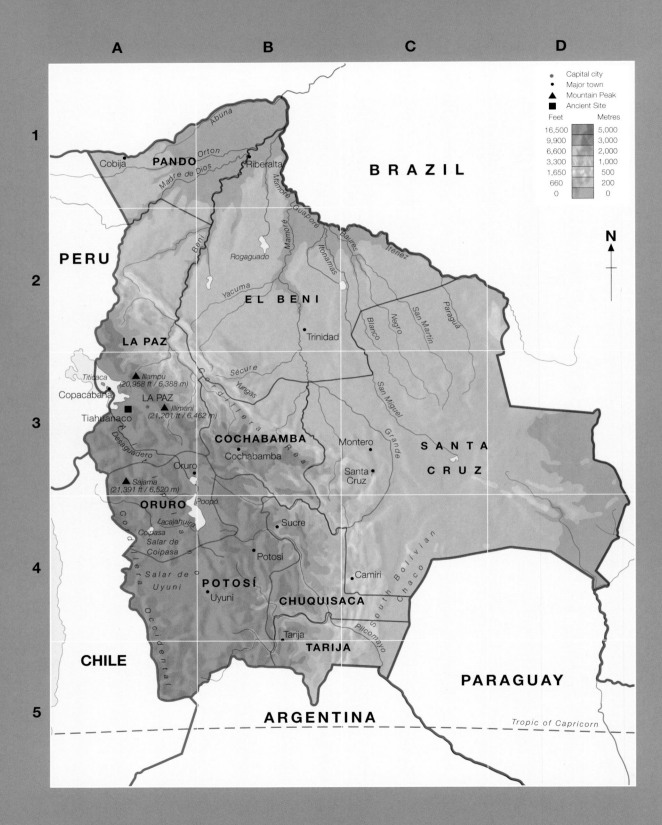

A   B   C   D

Capital city
Major town
▲ Mountain Peak
■ Ancient Site

Feet	Metres
16,500	5,000
9,900	3,000
6,600	2,000
3,300	1,000
1,650	500
660	200
0	0

N

BRAZIL

PERU

Abuná

Orton

Cobija

PANDO

Madre de Dios

Riberalta

Mamoré

Guaporé

Beni

Rogaguado

Itonamas

Baures

Iténez

EL BENI

Yacuma

Paraguá

Blanco

Negro

San Martín

Trinidad

LA PAZ

Sécure

Titicaca

▲ *Illampu*
(20,958 ft / 6,388 m)

San Miguel

Copacabana

LA PAZ

Yungas

▲ *Illimani*
(21,201 ft / 6,462 m)

Tiahuanaco

Desaguadero

Cordillera Real

COCHABAMBA

Grande

Montero

SANTA

Cochabamba

Santa
Cruz

CRUZ

Oruro

▲ *Sajama*
(21,391 ft / 6,520 m)

Poopó

ORURO

Lacajahuira

Coipasa

Sucre

Salar de
Coipasa

Potosí

Cordillera Occidental

Salar de
Uyuni

POTOSÍ

Camiri

South Bolivian Chaco

Uyuni

CHUQUISACA

Tarija

Pilcomayo

TARIJA

CHILE

PARAGUAY

ARGENTINA

Tropic of Capricorn

ECONOMIC BOLIVIA

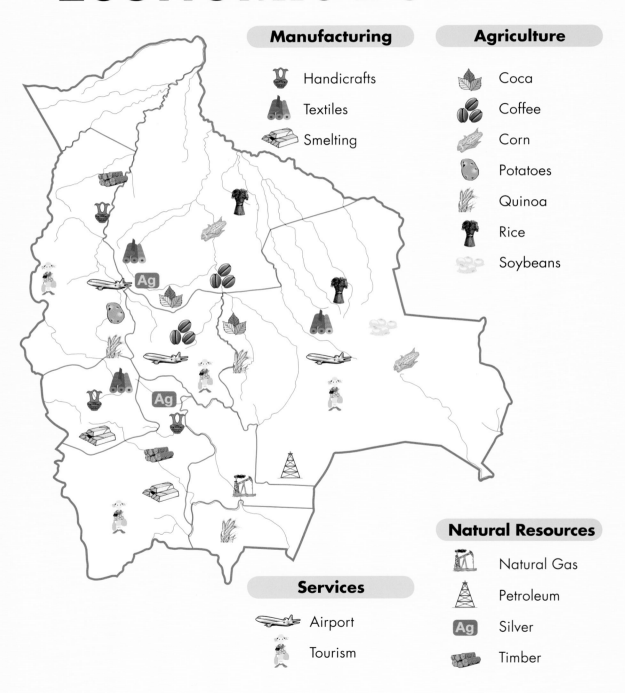

Manufacturing
- Handicrafts
- Textiles
- Smelting

Agriculture
- Coca
- Coffee
- Corn
- Potatoes
- Quinoa
- Rice
- Soybeans

Natural Resources
- Natural Gas
- Petroleum
- Ag Silver
- Timber

Services
- Airport
- Tourism

ABOUT
THE ECONOMY

OVERVIEW

During the Spanish colonial period Bolivia became a mere producer of raw materials for Spain, neglecting local needs. Sorely needed for a dynamic economy was the elaboration of raw materials into value-added products. Following independence, the Creole class merely continued the dependent export economy, with mining as the core. The Bolivian oligarchy was well trained by the colonial power to act as an intermediary rather than an independent producer. Much of today's impoverishment is due to the vestiges of the truncated economy. Since the 1990s, social movements have fought for a more independent and self-sufficient economy, and the government elected in 2005 is well aware of the need for natural resources to be transformed into value-added products.

INFLATION RATE

5.4 percent (2005 estimate)

CURRENCY

1 boliviano (BOB) = 100 cents
Notes: 2, 5, 10, 20, 50, 100, 200 BOB
Coins: 1 BOB; 2, 5, 10, 20, 50 cents
USD 1 = 7.99 bolivianos (March 2006)

GROSS DOMESTIC PRODUCT (GDP)

$23.59 billion (2005 estimate)

GDP PER CAPITA

$2,700 (2005 estimate)

GDP BY SECTOR

Agriculture 12.6 percent, industry 35 percent, services 52.4 percent (2005 estimates)

WORKFORCE

4.22 million (2005 estimate)

UNEMPLOYMENT RATE

8 percent (in urban areas); but widespread under-employment (2005 estimate)

INVESTMENTS

12.5 percent of GDP (2005 estimate)

AGRICULTURE PRODUCTS

Soybeans, coffee, coca, corn, sugarcane, quinoa, rice, potatoes, cotton, timber.

INDUSTRIAL PRODUCTS

Petroleum, mining, smelting, foodstuffs, beverages, tobacco, handicrafts, clothing.

EXPORT PARTNERS

Brazil, United States, Colombia, Peru, Japan.

IMPORT PARTNERS

Brazil, Argentina, United States, Chile, Peru.

CULTURAL BOLIVIA

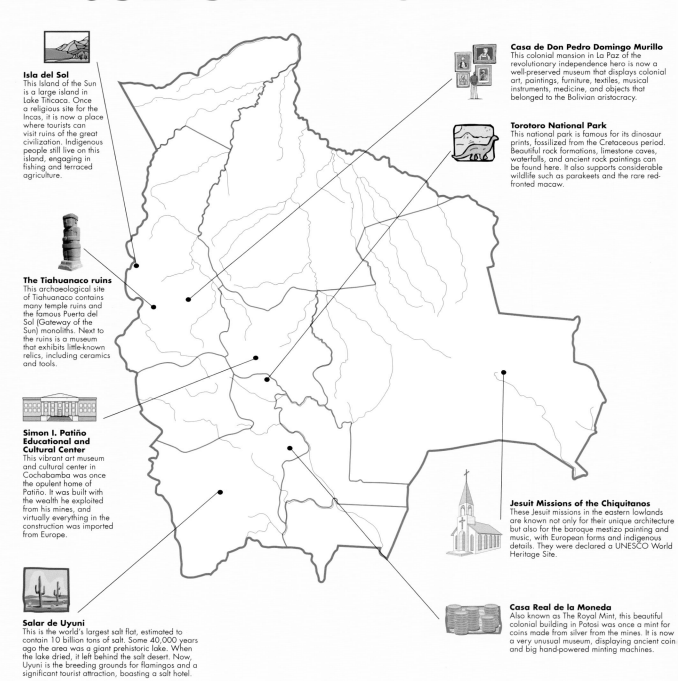

Isla del Sol
This Island of the Sun is a large island in Lake Titicaca. Once a religious site for the Incas, it is now a place where tourists can visit ruins of the great civilization. Indigenous people still live on this island, engaging in fishing and terraced agriculture.

The Tiahuanaco ruins
This archaeological site of Tiahuanaco contains many temple ruins and the famous Puerta del Sol (Gateway of the Sun) monoliths. Next to the ruins is a museum that exhibits little-known relics, including ceramics and tools.

Simon I. Patiño Educational and Cultural Center
This vibrant art museum and cultural center in Cochabamba was once the opulent home of Patiño. It was built with the wealth he exploited from his mines, and virtually everything in the construction was imported from Europe.

Salar de Uyuni
This is the world's largest salt flat, estimated to contain 10 billion tons of salt. Some 40,000 years ago the area was a giant prehistoric lake. When the lake dried, it left behind the salt desert. Now, Uyuni is the breeding grounds for flamingos and a significant tourist attraction, boasting a salt hotel.

Casa de Don Pedro Domingo Murillo
This colonial mansion in La Paz of the revolutionary independence hero is now a well-preserved museum that displays colonial art, paintings, furniture, textiles, musical instruments, medicine, and objects that belonged to the Bolivian aristocracy.

Torotoro National Park
This national park is famous for its dinosaur prints, fossilized from the Cretaceous period. Beautiful rock formations, limestone caves, waterfalls, and ancient rock paintings can be found here. It also supports considerable wildlife such as parakeets and the rare red-fronted macaw.

Jesuit Missions of the Chiquitanos
These Jesuit missions in the eastern lowlands are known not only for their unique architecture but also for the baroque mestizo painting and music, with European forms and indigenous details. They were declared a UNESCO World Heritage Site.

Casa Real de la Moneda
Also known as The Royal Mint, this beautiful colonial building in Potosi was once a mint for coins made from silver from the mines. It is now a very unusual museum, displaying ancient coin and big hand-powered minting machines.

ABOUT THE CULTURE

OFFICIAL NAME
Republic of Bolivia

AREA
424,165 square miles (1,098,581 square km)

CAPITAL
La Paz (seat of government); Sucre (legal capital and seat of judiciary)

DEPARTMENTS
Chuquisaca, Cochabamba, Beni, La Paz, Oruro, Pando, Potosí, Santa Cruz, Tarija

MAJOR LAKES
Lake Titicaca, Lake Poopó

MAJOR RIVERS
Beni, Mamoré, Desaguadero, Pilcomayo, Paraguay

HIGHEST POINT
Mount Sajama 21,391 feet (6,519 m)

POPULATION
8,857,870 (2005 estimate)

POPULATION IN MAJOR CITIES
Santa Cruz: 1,135,526
La Paz: 793,293
Cochabamba: 517,024
Sucre: 215,778
Oruro: 215,660
Potosí: 145,057 (2005 estimates)

LIFE EXPECTANCY
Approximately 65.5 years;
Men 62.89 years, women 68.25 years

ETHNIC GROUPS
Quechua 30 percent, mestizo (mixed white and indigenous ancestry) 30 percent, Aymará 25 percent, white 15 percent

OFFICIAL LANGUAGES
Spanish, Quechua, Aymará

NATIONAL ANTHEM
"National Hymn of Bolivia"

PRESIDENT
Evo Morales Ayma (2005–)

LITERACY RATE
Approximately 87.4 percent;
Men 93.1 percent, women 81.6 percent

MAJOR RELIGION
Roman Catholic 95 percent

TIME LINE

IN BOLIVIA	IN THE WORLD

A.D. 500–800
Tiahuanaco civilization emerged.

A.D. 600
Height of Mayan civilization

1000
The Chinese perfect gunpowder and begin to use it in warfare.

1476–1532
Height of the Incan civilization.

1530
Beginning of transatlantic slave trade organized by the Portuguese in Africa.

1538
The Spanish conquer Bolivia. Beginning of almost 300 years of colonial rule.

1544
Silver is discovered in Potosí. Plundering of the region and exploitation of indigenous labor becomes rampant.

1558–1603
Reign of Elizabeth I of England

1620
Pilgrims sail the *Mayflower* to America.

1776
U.S. Declaration of Independence

1781
Tupac Katari and Bartolina Sisa lead indigenous rebellion.

1789–99
The French Revolution

1809
Insurrection led by Pedro Domingo Murillo at La Paz crushed by the Spanish.

1825
Bolivia becomes independent.

1861
The U.S. Civil War begins.

1879–83
Pacific War with Chile. Bolivia loses its coast to Chile and becomes landlocked.

1899–1903
Arce War with Brazil. Bolivia loses more territories.

1914
World War I begins.

1932–35
Chaco War with Paraguay for supposed oil-rich territory. Bolivia loses the war but no oil was found there.

1939
World War II begins.

1945
The United States drops atomic bombs on Hiroshima and Nagasaki.

IN BOLIVIA	IN THE WORLD
	1949
	The North Atlantic Treaty Organization (NATO) is formed.
1952	
Revolution by peasants and miners. The MNR, led by Víctor Paz Estenssoro, takes power.	
	1957
	The Russians launch Sputnik.
1964	
Military coup by Vice President René Barrietos.	**1966–69**
1967	The Chinese Cultural Revolution
Ernesto Che Guevara is assassinated in Bolivia.	
1971	
Military coup by Hugo Bánzer Suárez.	
1971	
Military coup by Luis García Meza.	
1982	
Democracy is reestablished.	
1985	
Paz Estenssoro becomes president again and enacts economic reforms.	**1986**
1989	Nuclear power disaster at Chernobyl in Ukraine
Jaime Paz Zamora becomes president in coalition with longtime enemy Hugo Bánzer Suárez.	**1991**
1993	Breakup of the Soviet Union
Gonzálo Sánchez de Lozada becomes president.	
1997	**1997**
Former dictator Hugo Bánzer Suárez elected president.	Hong Kong is returned to China.
2000	
Water War breaks out. Social conflict in Bolivia.	**2001**
	Terrorists crash planes in New York, Washington, D.C., and Pennsylvania.
2002	
Gonzálo Sánchez is elected president again.	
2003	**2003**
Gas War. President Sánchez is forced to resign.	War in Iraq starts.
2005	
Evo Morales wins election, becoming the first indigenous president in Bolivian history.	

GLOSSARY

Altiplano (ahl-tee-PLAH-noh)
Also known as the High Plateau, a large expanse of high, flat land between two ranges of the Andes.

amautu (ah-MOW-too)
Wise men who traditonally memorized vast amounts of information.

ayni (AYE-nee)
A social system in which men of the village make decisions communally.

bombín (bohm-BEEN)
Bolivian name for a bowler hat, frequently worn by indigenous highland women.

campesino (kam-pay-SEE-noh)
A peasant or small-scale farmer. Since 1952, the official term for indigenous peoples.

cha'lla (CHAH-ya)
A ritual blessing, frequently drawn from a combination of Christian and indigenous beliefs.

chaqueo (cha-KAY-oh)
Burning fields to prepare for farming, a process that causes air pollution.

chulla (CHOO-lah)
A woolen knit hat with ear flaps worn by indigenous men.

chuño (CHOO-nyoh)
Potatoes that have been frozen and then dried in the sun.

cucho (KOO-choh)
A ritual offering placed in the foundation of a new building.

El Tío (TEE-oh)
Literally "uncle," the name for the indigenous god of minerals, patron of miners.

manta (MAHN-Tah)
Shawl worn by indigenous highland women that can be folded to carry babies or other loads.

padrino (pah-DREE-noh)
Godparent.

quenas (KAY-nas)
Flutes made from reed pipes.

salteñas (sal-TAY-nyahs)
Spicy meat pies often eaten as a snack.

sobremesa (soh-bray-MAY-sah)
The after-lunch hour, when people talk.

soroche (so-ROH-shay)
Altitude sickness, a frequent problem in La Paz.

surazo (soo-RAH-zoh)
Cold winds that blow in from the Argentine pampas.

viernes de soltero
(VYAIR-nays day sol-TAY-roh)
Literally "single on Friday," the Hispanic custom for men to go out without their wives on Friday nights to drink and play dice.

FURTHER INFORMATION

BOOKS

Ferry, Stephen (with essay by Eduardo Galeano). *I Am Rich Potosí: The Mountain That Eats Men.* New York: Monacelli Press, 1999.

Guevara, Ernesto Che (Introduction by Camilo Guevara and Fidel Castro). *The Bolivian Diary.* Melbourne, Australia: Ocean Press, 2005.

Olivera, Oscar and Lewis, Tom. *Cochabamba! Water Rebellion in Bolivia.* Cambridge, MA: South End Press, 2004.

WEB SITES

BBC News—with links to Bolivian press. http://news.bbc.co.uk/1/hi/world/americas/country_profiles/1210487.stm

CIA World Factbook. www.cia.gov/cia/publications/factbook/geos/bl.html

FILMS

La Sangre del Cóndor. Directed by Jorge Sanginés. Grupo Ukamau, 1969.

Cuestión de Fe. Directed by Marcos Loayza. Iconoscopio, 1995.

MUSIC

30 Años Solo Vive Una Vez. Los Kjarkas. Mambo Maniacs, 2003. (Bolivian folk music)

Nunca más! Atajo. Pro Audio, 2003. (Rock, blues, and folk fusion)

BIBLIOGRAPHY

Lonely Planet: Bolivia. Victoria, Australia: Lonely Planet Publications, 2001.

Murphy, Alan. *Bolivia Handbook.* Third edition. Bath, U.K.: Footprint Handbooks, 2002.

Sólon, Pablo. *La Otra Cara de la Historia.* La Paz, Bolivia: Fundacion Solon, 1999.

Bolivia dot com. www.bolivia.com

Bolivian Press. www.bolpress.com

Earth Trends: *Biodiversity and Protected Areas—Bolivia.* http://earthtrends.wri.org/pdf_library/
country_profiles/bio_cou_068.pdf

Embajada de Bolivia. www.embajadadebolivia.com.ar/medcomu.htm

Encyclopedia of the nations. www.nationsencyclopedia.com/Americas/Bolivia-ENVIRONMENT.html

FAN: Foundation for Friends of Nature. Bolivia. www.fan-bo.org

FOBOMADE. www.fobomade.org.bo/index1.php

General Secretariat of the Andean Community. www.comunidadandina.org/desarrollo/T2_d3.htm

Icomos. www.icomos.org/usicomos/Publications/Newsletters/1998_Issues/1998_No_4.htm#illicit

La Razón. www.la-razon.com

Mongabay. http://rainforests.mongabay.com/deforestation/2000/Bolivia.htm

Mongabay. http://news.mongabay.com/2005/0907-wwf.html

Official Bolivian government Web site. www.bolivia.gov.bo

Official Bolivian statistics Web site. www.ine.gov.bo

Peace Corps. www.peacecorps.gov

Tahuichi. www.tahuichi.com

The Progressive Magazine. Eduardo Galeano, "Bolivia: The Country that Wants to Exist."
www.progressive.org

World Wildlife Fund. www.wwf.fi/wwf/www/uploads/pdf/glaciersraportti.pdf

INDEX